OLD SONGS, NEW DISCOVERIES

Folk Song Papers, No. 2

Old Songs, New Discoveries

Selected Papers from the 2018 Folk Song Conference

Edited by
STEVE ROUD and DAVID ATKINSON

LONDON
THE BALLAD PARTNERS
2019

Published by
The Ballad Partners
19 Bedford Road
London N2 9DB
theballadpartners.co.uk

ISBN 978-1-9161424-1-1

Printed and bound by Biddles Books Ltd, Castle House, East Winch Road, Blackborough End, King's Lynn, Norfolk PE32 1SF.

The Ballad Partners is a not-for-profit cooperative venture established with the aims of:
• publishing, or facilitating the publication of, essays, conference proceedings, and other materials in the subjects of folk and traditional song, music, dance, custom (the 'folk arts'), street literature, and related fields
• raising awareness and encouraging the study of the folk arts via publication of suitable materials and their subsequent sale and distribution.
The Ballad Partners may also organize or support other activities, such as conferences, meetings, exhibitions, and displays, the purpose of which is to encourage research or to disseminate information in the subject areas listed above.
To become a subscriber please contact: info@theballadpartners.co.uk.

Folk Song Papers, No. 2

Folk Song Papers, No. 1 was published under the title *Proceedings of the English Folk Dance and Song Society Conference 2013* (edited by David Atkinson and Steve Roud) by CAMSCO Music and Loomis House Press in 2015, and is available from the EFDSS.

Contents

Preface

Despite the current lack of academic institutions with courses specializing in traditional music, research into traditional song is thriving. With branches stretching into a multitude of different disciplines – ethnomusicology, social history, folklore, anthropology, and so on – folk song is still being explored by academics and scholars as well as expert enthusiasts. However, this research may go un-noticed or may not get the exposure it deserves.

Over the past few years, through collaboration with organizations such as the Traditional Song Forum, the English Folk Dance & Song Society (EFDSS) has been keen to spotlight this research and to provide networking opportunities by arranging and hosting a series of conferences covering traditional song, music, and dance. Our 2018 conference 'Traditional Folk Song: Past, Present, and Future' was certainly successful at bringing together many facets of folk song – from historic sources in the radical press of the early nineteenth century, through the work of revivalists and nationalists like Marjory Kennedy-Fraser and A. L. Lloyd, to considerations of how traditional song continues to inspire and move people today, both as collectors and as performers in local folk clubs. There is more to explore, and by providing a platform for new research to be shared and discussed we hope to encourage further work in this fascinating subject area.

We also appreciate that in order for this research to develop and to be built upon the output from these conferences needs to be recorded in a permanent form. Hence the EFDSS is delighted to be working with the Ballad Partners to present and publish this selection of papers from the 2018 conference. We found the papers inspirational, and I hope that you, the reader, will do so too.

Laura Smyth
Library and Archives Director, English Folk Dance & Song Society

• Abbreviations used in this volume:

Roud Folk Song Index https://www.vwml.org/.
VWML: London, Vaughan Williams Memorial Library
https://www.vwml.org/.

• All online citations were accessed and verified on 21 June 2019.

Marjory Kennedy-Fraser (1857–1930): Musician, Musicologist, Suffragette, and Promoter of Scottish National Identity

PER AHLANDER

Early in October 1928, Marjory Kennedy-Fraser boarded the train in Edinburgh, travelling via Berlin to Prague where she was to represent Scotland at a congress of popular arts. In 1922, with the aim of reviving and developing the various national pre-war efforts, the International Committee on Intellectual Co-operation had been appointed by the League of Nations, and three years later the International Institute of Intellectual Co-operation, governed by the Committee, opened its offices in the Palais Royal in Paris. Most of the funding came from France, but there were also subsidies from Poland and Czechoslovakia.[1] High on the agenda was an international conference and it was decided to hold the first ever *Congrès international des arts populaires* in Prague from 7 to 13 October 1928.

The invitations met with a large response and around three hundred delegates from all over the world made their way to the Czechoslovak capital: 'Of these, some 50 were from Great Britain, largely camp followers and members of the English Folk-Dance Society, while Scotland was represented by myself, my daughter, and my sister. It was in the early spring that M. A[rnold] van Gennep, from Paris (conseiller scientifique du secrétariat général), had visited Scotland in search of representatives and had asked for our collaboration.'[2]

Kennedy-Fraser had written to Elizabeth Haldane about her plans in a letter of 23 September 1928:

---

[1] *International Institute of Intellectual Cooperation* (Paris: League of Nations, 1926), pp. 1–11, addendum.

[2] Marjory Kennedy-Fraser, Mus. Doc., C.B.E., 'Folk-Art: The Prague Congress', *Scotsman*, 3 November 1928, p. 14. See also 'International Congress of Popular Arts', *Journal of the English Folk Dance Society*, 2nd ser., 2 (1928), 49–52 (p. 49): 'Thirty-one nations were represented at the Congress. The English delegation, consisting for the most part of members of the English Folk Dance Society, formed the largest national contingent.'

Dear Miss Haldane,

I know that you, like your late brother, Lord Haldane, were always interested in International good feeling. I was asked to represent Scotland at the forthcoming League of Nations (Intellectual section) Folk Art Congress at Prague and thought it worth while to include Berlin and Vienna also. In Vienna the 'Kulturbund' is introducing us, in Berlin we are giving a recital at our own risk.

International exchange of traditional song may be the one touch of nature that makes the whole world kin.[3]

Despite participating in a congress promoting intellectual cooperation, there was not much unity within the British delegation and the English and Scottish sections did not work together – which is the more remarkable considering that Marjory Kennedy-Fraser's nephew, Douglas Kennedy, and his sister-in-law, Maud Karpeles, headed the substantial contingent from the English Folk Dance Society.[4] For one thing, relations were strained between Kennedy and Karpeles.[5] Furthermore, as subsequently pointed out in the monthly journal of the International Institute of Intellectual Cooperation, 'L'art populaire est, en effet, souvent beaucoup plus régional que national' ('Popular art is indeed often more regional than national').[6]

While the Scots recital was featured as the finale of the official congress banquet, held in the Obecní dům, the English participants had invited congress delegates to their public performance earlier in the week, 'by [which] means opportunity was afforded of showing the wealth and diversity of the Society's *répertoire*'.[7] The show took place on 11 October at the Sophieninsel (Slovanský ostrov): 'Das ganze Programm wird durch Londoner Künstler und Mitglieder der "The english Folk Dance Society" ausgeführt' ('The entire programme will be performed by London artists and members of "The English Folk Dance Society"').[8]

---

[3] Edinburgh, National Library of Scotland, MS 6034, ff. 103–04, Kennedy-Fraser to Elizabeth Haldane, 23 September 1928.

[4] 'International Congress of Popular Arts', p. 50.

[5] Michael Heaney, 'Kennedy, Douglas Neil (1893–1988)', *Oxford Dictionary of National Biography* https://doi.org/10.1093/ref:odnb/54871.

[6] Richard Dupierreux, 'Les arts populaires et l'esprit international', *La coopération intellectuelle*, 1.1 (15 January 1929), 15–17 (p. 15).

[7] 'International Congress of Popular Arts', p. 50 (the Scottish recital at the official banquet is not mentioned).

[8] 'Kunst – Buch – Kultur', *Prager Tagblatt*, 11 October 1928, p. 7; see also 'Kunst – Buch – Kultur', *Prager Tagblatt*, 10 October 1928, p. 8.

By kind permission of Edinburgh University Library.

The proceedings of the Prague congress were published in 1931 in two large, beautifully illustrated volumes, introduced by Sorbonne professor Henri Focillon and exquisitely printed in Brussels for Éditions Duchartre, but by that time Kennedy-Fraser had been dead for a year and no Scottish material was included.[9] When the second *Congrès international des arts populaires* was held in Antwerp, Liège, and

---

[9] Institut international de coopération intellectuelle, *Art populaire: Travaux artistiques et scientifiques du 1er Congrès international des arts populaires, Prague 1928*, introd. Henri Focillon, 2 vols (Paris: Éditions Duchartre, 1931).

Brussels, also in 1931, both Scotland and Wales had entirely vanished from the agenda.[10]

Marjory Kennedy-Fraser, born in Perth in 1857 as Marjory Kennedy, was most certainly Scottish, but, like many other Scots over the centuries, maintaining both a Scottish and a British identity never seemed a problem for her. Moreover, after moving to London with her family at the age of five, and thus spending her formative years in the British capital, she also developed an English identity, and although she lived in Edinburgh for most of her adult life she would always feel at home in London.[11]

Her father, David Kennedy (1825–86), was a well-known Scottish tenor who became internationally famous for his renderings of Lowland Scots songs, a repertoire centred upon the works of Robert Burns and performed with piano accompaniments in concert halls and similar venues in the style of the period. In possession of a solid bel canto technique, Mr Kennedy could undoubtedly have made a successful career in opera, but instead he chose to devote his entire professional life to performing the songs of Scotland – in the British Isles, throughout the Empire, and in the United States. He made his London debut at the prestigious Hanover Square Rooms in 1862, and after over one hundred recitals at various London venues he settled there for a couple of years with his growing family while consolidating his career. Starting out performing professionally he worked with the then well-known pianist Edward Land (1815–76), but by the summer of 1870 his thirteen-year-old daughter Marjory had become fully established as her father's accompanist, a position she would hold for the next seventeen years until his untimely death in Canada in 1886. Besides playing for her father, she would regularly perform as a singer in their family concerts, both in ensembles and as a soloist, thus gaining an exceptional in-depth knowledge of the repertoire of vocal and instrumental Lowland Scottish music.

Between 1866 and 1886 the Kennedys toured widely, both at home and around the world. While compiling listings of the vast amount of music performed by the Kennedys during these two

---

[10] For an overview of the interlinked international organizations, cf. Bjarne Rogan, 'The Prague Congress (1928), CIAP and the League of Nations: A Short History of La commission internationale des arts populaires (CIAP) from its Inception until World War II', in *Everyday Life and Cultural Patterns: International Festschrift for Elle Vunder*, ed. Ene Kõresaar and Art Leete (Tartu: Tartu University Press, 2004), pp. 284–302. I am indebted to Derek Schofield for drawing my attention to this essay.

[11] Per G. L. Ahlander 'Marjory Kennedy-Fraser (1857–1930) and her Time: A Contextual Study' (unpublished doctoral thesis, University of Edinburgh, 2009).

decades, it became very noticeable how their repertoire evolved from a ragbag of Scottish songs, popular British hits, and European light classics, to almost exclusively Scottish material by the end of the period.[12] There may have been several different reasons for this gradual shift in choice of concert repertoire. In a way, they went with the flow, as this was a time when an interest in national heritage was in vogue generally – in the wake of the waves of nationalism that had swept over large areas of Europe there was a fascination with the individual European nations' origins and traditions. Scotland was particularly rich in this respect and ever since the Ossianic fever some hundred years earlier its rugged landscape and mythical past had fascinated Europe. After having become firmly established among the top performers in their genre, the Kennedys presumably also felt secure enough to focus on the kind of repertoire they longed for, leaving out the standard pieces that would have been performed by most artistes of the era.

Politically aware, the Kennedys were steadfast Liberals and ardent supporters of British prime minister W. E. Gladstone and his Irish Home Rule ambitions. While touring the Empire they came to appreciate the egalitarian societies in Australia and New Zealand, while strongly disapproving of the prevalent unequal social conditions in British India, where they were often deeply shocked and disgusted by how their compatriots treated their Indian subordinates. Marjory was never part of the Kennedys' tour of British India, however.

Apart from promoting his own career in order to earn a decent living, it is difficult to say to what extent David Kennedy had any further ambitions at the outset other than a clear wish to bring the songs of Scotland to his countrymen in the diaspora. Over the years, however, his efforts to reinforce the Scots' separate cultural and national identity within the British Empire became increasingly apparent. The Scottish culture and identity referred to here was the mainstream image of all things Scottish: Robert Burns, Jacobite songs, and the Scots language – Lowland Scots culture, in essence. The cultural heritage of the *Gàidhealtachd*, the Gaelic-speaking parts of the Scottish Highlands, was never part of David Kennedy's mission and consequently, for the time being at least, not of his daughter's either.

Marjory Kennedy-Fraser thus grew up surrounded by political discussion and it is not difficult to see how her social and political

---

[12] Per G. L. Ahlander, 'Taking "Twa Hours at Hame" to the New World: The Overseas Tours of David Kennedy's Family Music Troupe in 1866–86', *Review of Scottish Culture*, 25 (2013), 97–136.

views were formed at an early age. Furthermore, having herself had the good fortune to be raised in an environment where men and women could develop their skills on equal terms, she must soon have realized that that was the exception rather than the rule in an era when women were not even entitled to vote. Seen in this light, it seems only natural that she would become involved in the suffragette movement when it gained momentum at the beginning of the twentieth century.

In between their many concert tours, Marjory managed to squeeze in a few years of full-time music study in Milan, followed by some time spent at Mathilde Marchesi's private singing school in Paris in 1882. She may not have benefited much vocally from her studies with Marchesi, but she certainly enjoyed the multilingual atmosphere in her Parisian studio and the familiarity it gave her with the top-level international singing tuition of the period. Later in life she would refer to those months in Paris as 'a turning-point in [her] life',[13] as the linguistic variety she had experienced there had made her reflect upon her own Scottish background. On 10 February 1922, in a lecture on 'Songs of the Hebrides' at the Forum Club's Music Section in London, she said:

> In 1882 I was studying with Mathilde Marchesi, the famous singing teacher, in Paris in a cosmopolitan crowd of students who sang in all the European languages and on my return to Scotland in the summer of that year it occurred to me that there was a second language in my own country which might be worthy of a singer's attention so I there and then proceeded to study the Scots Gaelic and indeed to sing it (with my sisters and my father D. K. [David Kennedy] the Scots singer) round and round the world.[14]

The Forum Club, at 6 Grosvenor Place, established in 1919 as the London Centre for Women's Institute members, was one of the many upmarket clubs for women formed from about 1900.[15]

Back home in Edinburgh she decided to take up singing in Gaelic, the language of her ancestors. She did not know any Gaelic herself at that time, but Charles Fraser, her maternal grandfather, had spoken only Gaelic in his youth. However, he absolutely refused to give his

---

[13] Marjory Kennedy-Fraser, *A Life of Song* (London: Oxford University Press, 1929), p. 78.

[14] Edinburgh University Library, Gen. 284, Marjory Kennedy-Fraser, 'Songs of the Hebrides', lecture at the Forum Club's Music Section, London, 10 February 1922.

[15] Elizabeth Crawford, *The Women's Suffrage Movement: A Reference Guide, 1866–1928* (London and New York: Routledge, 2001), pp. 117–18, 120.

granddaughter any Gaelic coaching, having been much ridiculed on account of his native language during his youth. Eventually, while on tour in Scotland later in 1882, she met a man in Grantown-on-Spey who was able to teach her the basics of the language.[16]

Scottish Gaeldom and the Gaelic language were at an all-time low in those years, considered both backward and culturally barren. This was the result of several factors working in the same direction. There had been mass emigration from the Gaelic-speaking heartlands, either to Scotland's industrialized Central Belt or overseas, caused by a combination of overpopulation, famine, and the infamous evictions – a direct consequence of the large landowners' decisions to clear their estates of what they considered unprofitable crofters in order to make room for the much more lucrative sheep-grazing business. There was also a perceived connection between Gaelic culture and Ireland and Catholicism, which was frowned upon in austere Presbyterian Scotland.

The Gaelic language, although still spoken by the majority of those living in the Hebrides and in the western part of the Scottish Highlands, had thus come under increasing pressure. Even if the language had been on the decline for a very long time in Scotland as a whole, it had nonetheless remained the mother tongue of the rural population in the Gaelic heartland. However, following the implementation of the 1872 Education (Scotland) Act, when English became the only language to be used in education, and monoglot Gaelic-speaking children were taught by monoglot English-speaking teachers in primary schools, the decline of the Gaelic language accelerated rapidly.

At the same time, there was a surge of interest in the ancient tongue among the literati. There were Gaelic Societies in both Inverness and London, where many Scots enjoyed successful careers and had become interested in the cultural heritage of their ancestors. Nostalgia may have played a part, but probably also the general fascination with everything Scottish – epitomized by Queen Victoria's acquisition of Balmoral Castle in the 1850s and her craze for tartan. In Scotland, after much canvassing, the first Celtic chair was created at the University of Edinburgh in 1882. Thus we have a language that was considered a nuisance in the areas where it was still spoken, and at the same time the upper echelons of society were beginning to take an antiquarian interest in it, mainly in the larger urban areas where Gaelic had never been part of the sociological infrastructure.

---

[16] Kennedy-Fraser, *A Life of Song*, p. 78.

At that time, Logan & Co. in Inverness were publishing a series of volumes of Gaelic songs and Marjory Kennedy arranged some of them 'as unaccompanied trios for three equal voices',[17] and sang them with her sisters Helen and Margaret. David Kennedy was very positive about his daughter's idea of introducing 'the Gaelic tongue on the concert platform', even though he almost never ventured to sing in Gaelic himself. From then on, most of their recitals around the world were to include some Gaelic songs, performed by 'The Misses Kennedy'.[18] Both the Gaelic trios and the ensemble singing were greatly appreciated wherever they went, according to contemporary press reviews.

The 'Songs of Scotland' tours came to an abrupt halt when David Kennedy died in 1886, and Marjory then settled in Edinburgh, where she married Alec Fraser (1857–90), a Scottish mathematician, later a headmaster in Glasgow, with whom she had two children, David and Patuffa. Widowed after less than four years of marriage, she read music at the University of Edinburgh under Professor Frederick Niecks as one of the institution's very first women students, and launched a successful singing and piano-teaching career in both Edinburgh and Glasgow.

Establishing herself as a self-supporting and successful urban professional in Edinburgh's artistic avant-garde circles, she met John Stuart Blackie, Alexander Carmichael, Patrick Geddes, John Duncan,

---

[17] Marjory Kennedy arranged several songs for three female voices. The following thirty-one trios are preserved in manuscript in a black quarto music book, stamped T. Claxton, Music Dealer, Toronto: 'Fear a' bhàta', 'Mo nighean donn bhoidheach', 'Fionn airidh', 'Gu ma slan a chi mi', 'Mairi Laghach', 'Maighdeann Mhuile', 'Mo run geal dìleas', 'Moladh na Landaibh', 'Is toigh leam a' Ghàidhealtachd', 'Gabhaidh sinn an Eathar mor', 'An Ribhinn Donn', 'Braw, Braw Lads', 'I'm Ower Young', 'The Boatie Rows', 'Kirkconnell Lea', 'Hey the Bonnie Breast-Knots', 'Comin' thro' the Rye', 'The Broom o' the Cowdenknowes', 'Thou Hast Left Me Ever, Jamie', 'Afton Water', 'The Yellow Haired Laddie', 'Duanag a Chiobair'/'Shepherds [sic] Lay', 'My Love's in Germany', 'Twa Bonnie Maidens', 'Gloomy Winter', 'Waly Waly', 'Soiridh'/ 'Farewell', 'Leis an Lurgainn'/'A Boat Song', 'Am Fleasgach Donn'/'The Brown Haired Lad', 'Faill ill o' agus ho ro eile', 'The Keel Row'.(Edinburgh University Library, Gen. 279). Published in 1923, Marjory Kennedy-Fraser, *The Kennedy-Fraser Collection of Scots Songs – Gaelic and Lowland: Arranged for Female Voices S.S.C.* (Glasgow: Paterson, 1923), is made up of nine separately printed songs, issued in both staff and sol-fa: 'Flora Macdonald's Lament', 'The High Road' ('Gabhaidh sinn an Rathad Mor'), 'Farewell to Fiunary' ('Fionn-Airidh'), 'Afton Water', 'The Broom o' the Cowdenknowes', 'My Nut-Brown Maiden' ('Mo Nighean donn Bhoidheach'), 'The Lonely Reaper' ('A Fhleasgaich Dhuinn'), 'My Love's in Germanie', 'Braw, Braw Lads'.

[18] Kennedy-Fraser, *A Life of Song*, p. 78.

and Phoebe Traquair – all leading lights of the Celtic Revival and the Arts and Crafts movement in Scotland. She lectured on the history of music and organized concerts at the polymath Patrick Geddes's Edinburgh Summer Meetings, and she worked as music critic for the *Edinburgh Evening News*, which was at the time the most widely circulated local newspaper. Deeply involved in Patrick Geddes's philanthropic work through the Edinburgh Social Union, she was elected parish councillor, mainly devoting herself to poor relief and to matters related to the welfare of women and children. Gradually, she was drawn into the women's suffrage movement, performing at their gatherings, speaking at their meetings, and taking part in their marches and parades in both Edinburgh and London – always, however, keeping well away from any of the illegal or violent actions for which the suffragettes have become notorious.

When Kennedy-Fraser first landed on the Hebridean island of Eriskay in 1905 it was at the instigation of her former Edinburgh Summer Meetings colleague, the painter John Duncan (1866–1945), whose portrait of her is now in the Scottish National Portrait Gallery.[19] She went there to note down the Gaelic songs that Duncan had overheard while painting on the island the previous summer, and she soon became very enthusiastic and realized that this was the perfect spot for song collecting. As mentioned above, she had become interested in Gaelic songs in the early 1880s, but since the death of her father, apart from giving talks on Celtic music at Geddes's Summer Meetings, the topic had lain dormant. Now, however, things were to change rapidly and over the years that followed she came to devote more and more of her time to the Hebridean songs.

When visiting the island in 1905 she noted down the songs 'entirely in manuscript', but once she was back in Edinburgh 'the people said, "Oh but Mrs Kennedy Fraser you've been writing these melodies yourself; you haven't found them."'[20] That was certainly one of the reasons why, when she returned to Eriskay in the summer of 1907, she took along an Edison Bell graphophone,[21] but 'also it saved

---

[19] Edinburgh, National Galleries of Scotland, John Duncan, *Marjory Kennedy Fraser, 1857–1930: Musician and Collector of Hebridean songs*, c.1922, oil on canvas, https://www.nationalgalleries.org/art-and-artists/2482/marjory-kennedy-fraser-1857-1930-musician-and-collector-hebridean-songs.

[20] Edinburgh, School of Scottish Studies Archives (SSA), SM 1965/11, transcription, p. 8.

[21] Percy Grainger, too, used a 'Standard' Edison-Bell Phonograph when collecting. See Percy Grainger, 'Collecting with the Phonograph', *Journal of the Folk-Song Society*, 3.3 (no. 12) (1908), 147–242 (p. 148). According to Patuffa Kennedy-Fraser, however,

time there because it was far quicker to make a record of a song than to try and write it down in paper and pencil'.[22] It was a 'very small and easily portable recording graphophone', she recalled in her autobiography some two decades later, with 'a good supply of wax cylindrical blank records. So now when we went down to the *ceilidhs* in the evening we could entertain the folk with the reproduction of their own voices while at the same time amassing valuable material for our work'.[23]

Although not the first in Britain to make use of recording equipment when collecting folk songs, Kennedy-Fraser was one of the pioneers.[24] Percy Grainger had made recordings in north Lincolnshire in July and August 1906; Lucy Broadwood used a phonograph in Arisaig, Scotland, in July 1907; and Cecil Sharp and Ralph Vaughan Williams made some cylinder recordings in the period 1907–09.[25] On the Continent, however, recordings were being made by the end of the nineteenth century, by Yevgeniya Linyova, who began recording polyphonic folk songs in the European part of Russia in 1897, and by Béla Bartók, who used the phonograph to collect folk music from 1906.[26]

Kennedy-Fraser undoubtedly wanted to document the Gaelic cultural heritage for posterity,[27] and had found crucial inspiration in

---

the recording apparatus was called a 'graphophone', not a 'phonograph' (SSA, SM 1965/11, transcription, p. 1). An Edison 'Gem' Phonograph and a Columbia Graphophone, together with two phonograph bells, were presented to the University of Edinburgh by Marjory Kennedy-Fraser.

[22] SSA, SM 1965/11, transcription, p. 8.

[23] Kennedy-Fraser, *A Life of Song*, p. 126.

[24] Francis Collinson, 'Songs of the Hebrides: Mrs Kennedy Fraser's Arrangements Left Trail of Confusion', *Scotsman*, 6 January 1958.

[25] Grainger, 'Collecting with the Phonograph'; Michael Yates, 'Percy Grainger and the Impact of the Phonograph', *Folk Music Journal*, 4.3 (1982), 265–75; Katherine Campbell, 'Lucy Broadwood and John Potts: A Collecting Episode in the Scottish Borders', *Folk Music Journal*, 9.2 (2007), 219–25.

[26] James Bailey and Mikhail Lobanov, 'A Collection of Translations of Russian Folk Songs: E. E. Lineva's Visit to America (1892–1896)', *Slavic and East European Folklore Association Journal*, 4.2 (1999), 24–34; Vera Lampert, 'Bartók at the Piano: Lessons from the Composer's Sound Recordings', in *The Cambridge Companion to Bartók*, ed. Amanda Bayley (Cambridge: Cambridge University Press, 2001), pp. 231–42. Phonograph recordings continued to be made in Lithuania (then in imperial Russia) in 1910–12. See Nijolė Sliužinskienė and Rimantas Sliužinskas, 'Folk Song in Lithuania', in *Folk Song: Tradition, Revival, and Re-Creation*, ed. Ian Russell and David Atkinson (Aberdeen: Elphinstone Institute, University of Aberdeen, 2004), pp. 53–66 (p. 55).

[27] Marjory Kennedy-Fraser donated her collection of wax cylinder recordings, together with her recording equipment, to the University of Edinburgh in 1930. Moreover, the University of Edinburgh Centre for Research Collections (CRC) holds

Louis Albert Bourgault-Ducoudray's *Trente mélodies populaires de Basse-Bretagne*.[28] She had grown up with Lowland Scots songs and poetry, but to date was no expert on Gaelic music. She may not have known exactly what to do with her rich harvest of material at the very start of her collecting career, but as a trained musician, well versed in the classical art song repertoire, she soon began to consider how best to introduce Gaelic songs to audiences used to more conventional recitals.

She started out by giving a few Hebridean recitals in Edinburgh and Glasgow, having composed suitable piano arrangements for the songs she had collected, somewhat in the style of Claude Debussy. A musician by profession, she mainly focused on the melodies, and not having noted down more than snippets of the Gaelic verses, she wrote her own English words to some of the songs, something she was to regret later in life. When she performed at the Pan-Celtic Congress held in Edinburgh in 1907, Alfred Perceval Graves was in the audience. He was very enthusiastic about what he heard and told London music publisher Arthur Boosey about the Hebridean songs. After a recital at another pan-Celtic gathering in London the following year, Boosey approached Kennedy-Fraser and offered to undertake the publication of a volume of *Songs of the Hebrides*.[29] In April 1908, the *Celtic Review* briefly mentioned that her work was 'to be issued in volume form by Boosey' – 'her songs of the Hebrides are exactly what they profess to be, showing a freshness and originality not to be found in versions edited into consonance with the artificial rules of alien musicians.'[30]

The first *Songs of the Hebrides* volume was published in London in 1909 (forty-five songs). It was edited and reprinted several times, and in 1917 a second volume appeared (fifty-three songs), followed by a

---

a vast collection of her working documents, manuscripts, proofs, letters, and photographs. My inventory of the Marjory Kennedy-Fraser Collection is at https://www.era.lib.ed.ac.uk/bitstream/handle/1842/21088/H1036.pdf.

[28] Louis Albert Bourgault-Ducoudray, *Trente mélodies populaires de Basse-Bretagne: Traduction française en vers par Fr. Coppée*, introd. Louis Albert Bourgault-Ducoudray (Paris: Henry Lemoine, 1885).

[29] Some of the songs were already engraved, since Marjory Kennedy-Fraser had published them separately at her own risk, and these were to be included in the volume Boosey undertook to publish. The engraved plates always remained in Kennedy-Fraser's possession (Kennedy-Fraser, *A Life of Song*, pp. 140–41; SSA, SM 1965/11, transcription, pp. 3–4.)

[30] 'Songs of the Hebrides', *Celtic Review*, 4 (15 April 1908), 379.

third (fifty-one songs) in 1921.[31] A fourth volume (forty-one songs) came out in Glasgow in 1926 through another publisher.[32] A fifth volume (eighteen songs) was published in London in 1929.[33] There were also various other publications based on the main ones, such as adaptations for schools and easy arrangements for drawing-room pianists. Additionally, there were two series of piano pieces, as well as arrangements for cello and piano. There were even a few pieces for organ, although not arranged by Kennedy-Fraser herself. Her more theoretical academic work, analysing and systematizing the musical components of the songs she had collected, is to be found mainly in her introductions to the different volumes of Hebridean songs, including an extensive musicological section, under the title 'Some Tunes from my Note Books of 1926–27 in the Outer Isles',[34] in the 1929 volume:

> Some years ago M. [Duhamel], the French expert in Franco-Celtic music, that of Brittany, begged me to set down every old Gaelic tune I came across for the use of the future *musicologue*, who might find therein support for his scale theories, etc.[35]

Over the years Kennedy-Fraser gradually evolved from focusing on musical matters to using the songs as a means to place the Gaels on the political agenda, in a manner akin to her father's progression from performing Lowland Scots songs to using them to reinforce a separate Scottish identity.

Kennedy-Fraser's wish to speak for the Gaels was by no means unique and was, indeed, fully in line with the *Zeitgeist* – the fascination with the separate cultural identities of different parts of Europe. As Donald Meek has noted, the specifically Scottish project of 'present[ing] the Gaels as a distinct *Kulturvolk*' was epitomized by the

---

[31] Marjory Kennedy-Fraser and Kenneth Macleod, *Songs of the Hebrides: Collected and Arranged for Voice and Pianoforte with Gaelic and English Words* (London: Boosey, 1909, 1917, 1921).

[32] Marjory Kennedy-Fraser and Kenneth Macleod, *From the Hebrides: Further Gleanings of Tale and Song* (Glasgow: Paterson, 1926).

[33] Marjory Kennedy-Fraser, *More Songs of the Hebrides* (London: Boosey, 1929).

[34] Her final draft of this section is in Edinburgh University Library, Gen. 281.

[35] Kennedy-Fraser, *More Songs of the Hebrides*, p. iv. Christopher MacLeod, *The Gaelic Music of the Hebrides: Its History and Structure* (Stornoway: C. MacLeod, 2002), p. 92, wrote in 2002: 'Marjory Kennedy-Fraser, in her collections of Gaelic music, states that there are Gaelic songs in every one of the modes. This is true, but to find them you must look very hard, the vast majority of tunes are written in three modes – The Dorian, the Mixolydian and the Ionian.'

Carmina Gadelica, the monumental lifetime achievement of Alexander Carmichael, with whom Kennedy-Fraser was well acquainted.[36] Although a seminal work in itself, the *Carmina Gadelica* appeared against the backdrop of the Celtic Revival, which sought its inspiration in a remote, somewhat idealized past of Celtic art, literature, and chivalry. The several *Songs of the Hebrides* volumes that Kennedy-Fraser brought out from 1909 onwards fit in extremely well with the ethos of the Celtic Revival. However, she also saw the possibility of creating something new – 'an art-song that should incorporate faithfully within itself our Scoto-Celtic melodic heritage'.[37] The editing of folk songs had by then become an everyday activity among many of her continental contemporaries, and the 'national schools' of European music had long since found a home for themselves in drawing rooms and concert halls. Her task was twofold, wrote Professor Donald Tovey of the University of Edinburgh in 1930: 'The songs of the Hebrides were first to be collected. Then they were to be published in settings that would find wide acceptance among music-lovers other than those who are disposed to confine their attention to primitive music.'[38]

If Kennedy-Fraser's observations relating to sociological and demographic matters were largely concordant with those of at least her more enlightened Scottish contemporaries, her approach to the music she heard in Eriskay was clearly more European than British. That is not surprising, considering how deeply influenced she was by musical developments on the Continent, in particular within the areas of opera and art song. When considered in relation to the extensive corpus of European art songs, it is remarkable how well the *Songs of the Hebrides* blend in with the many contemporary contributions to the genre. From the late nineteenth century onwards, several composers collected traditional music and made more or less authentic classical arrangements of the original material – Béla Bartók, Benjamin Britten, Joseph Canteloube, Antonín Dvořák, Percy Grainger, Edvard Grieg, Leoš Janáček, Zoltán Kodály, and Ralph Vaughan Williams are names that spring to mind. The *Songs of the Hebrides* arrangements represent a valuable contribution to this vast art song repertoire, but they do need to be considered in that context and not thought of as scholarly

---

[36] Donald E. Meek, 'Faking the "True Gael"? *Carmina Gadelica* and the Beginning of Modern Gaelic Scholarship', *AISTE: Rannsachadh air Litreachas Gàidhlig/ Studies in Gaelic Literature*, 1 (2007), 76–106 (pp. 84, 104).

[37] Kennedy-Fraser, *A Life of Song*, pp. 120–21.

[38] Donald F. Tovey, 'An Appreciation', *Scotsman*, 24 November 1930, p. 8.

accurate reproductions of what Kennedy-Fraser had collected during her many field trips.

In the Gaelic context, however, her work was indeed a new phenomenon, a fact that was clearly pointed out by An Comunn Gàidhealach in its tribute to her in 1930: 'She created art song which was a new creation. They could not stand exactly on one form. They developed a new form, and the new form which arose out of the beautiful Gaelic melodies was the art song.'[39] Writing about Kenneth Macleod (1871–1955), Kennedy-Fraser's Gaelic editor and long-time collaborator, Thomas Murchison observed in 1988 both that 'Never before had the world outside Gaeldom been so impressively and entrancingly made aware of the quantity and quality of Hebridean music', and that both Kennedy-Fraser and her collaborator 'had "processed" the "raw material" they used', which is something that was never concealed by either of them.[40] Kennedy-Fraser wrote in the introduction to the 1909 volume: 'We have provided English words, at times they are translations more or less literal, at times they are merely singing verses, good vocal syllables provided for singers who have not the opportunity to learn the pronunciation of the original.'[41]

In her ambition to show Gaelic culture as one of the many equally valuable and important components of Europe's cultural heritage, Kennedy-Fraser was indeed successful. Introducing the Gaelic songs to fashionable Edwardian audiences, even if somewhat provocative at first, in the end made her efforts both socially acceptable and highly esteemed. Influential individuals of the period were fascinated by the many songs and tales she published in collaboration with Kenneth Macleod, and they both 'did a lot to popularise a more positive view of Gaeldom and boost the self-confidence of a people who had been taught for generations that their culture was worthless'.[42] Her 'Songs of the Hebrides' recitals became regular features of the prestigious London music scene and throughout the British Isles, and she made several highly successful North American tours. Moreover, her recitals on the Continent, as well as her contacts with Breton nationalist and musicologist Maurice Duhamel (1884–1940), the author of *Les 15*

---

[39] 'An Comunn Gaidhealach: Tribute to Mrs Kennedy Fraser', *Scotsman*, 28 November 1930, p. 8.

[40] Thomas Moffatt Murchison, 'Introduction', in *Sgrìobhaidhean Choinnich MhicLeòid: The Gaelic Prose of Kenneth MacLeod*, ed. Thomas M. Murchison (Edinburgh: Scottish Academic Press for the Scottish Gaelic Texts Society, 1988), pp. i–xlv (pp. xxxiv–xxxv).

[41] Kennedy-Fraser and Macleod, *Songs of the Hebrides* (1909), p. xxi.

[42] Camille Dressler, *Eigg: The Story of an Island* (Edinburgh: Polygon, 1998), p. 107.

modes de la musique Bretonne,[43] and other continental authorities on folk song, made Hebridean music known and appreciated far beyond the Anglo-Saxon world. Over the years, her songs 'impressed thousands upon thousands of ordinary folk the world over, who, but for Mrs Kennedy Fraser's labours of love, would never have heard of Gaelic folk-music'.[44]

Apparently, her voice even found its way into Westminster. In July 1918, when the Scottish Grand Committee discussed an amendment to the Scottish Education Bill, 'providing for the inclusion of schemes for the teaching of Gaelic in Gaelic-speaking areas', Mr A. F. Whyte noted 'that Gaelic had a literature and a poetry of its own of great importance and great value at the present time and in all future time', and he 'should be prepared to base his case for the fostering of Gaelic on one point alone, namely, on the very remarkable collection of poems and melodies which Mrs Kennedy Fraser had collected in the past few years'.[45]

In 1914, when 'the War was upon us [. . .] we were artistically paralyzed for a time',[46] but she continued to give lecture-recitals throughout the war years, if less frequently than before. Financially, though, it was a difficult time for her: she lost her job as a music critic and experienced a considerable downturn in demand for private music tuition. The plethora of benefit concerts organized during the war did not provide musicians with much income, but at least gave them a chance to appear before an audience and to show their solidarity with the war effort. The Kennedy-Frasers were involved frequently, mainly in events that were in aid of Hebridean or, more generally, Gaelic and Highland purposes, or that were initiated by organizations within the women's suffrage movement. Marjory's daughter, Patuffa Kennedy-Fraser, performed at various charity events in London, where she studied music and lived with her uncle and aunt, Tobias and Jessie Matthay, the latter Marjory's youngest sister.

In 1915 Kennedy-Fraser took a fancy to a pipe tune and suggested that Kenneth Macleod, her Gaelic editor, write 'something "swanky" to that' – 'a tramping song for the Scots lads then "somewhere in France"'. So he did, and shortly afterwards she received from him

---

[43] Maurice Duhamel, *Les 15 modes de la musique Bretonne* (Paris: Rouart, Lerolle & Cie, 1911).

[44] Maurice Lindsay, '"Love and music will endure for ever" – Mrs Kennedy Fraser (1857–1930): Songs of the Hebrides', *Scottish Field*, 105 (no. 659) (1957), 42–44 (p. 44).

[45] 'Scottish Education Bill: The Teaching of Gaelic', *Scotsman*, 31 July 1918, p. 6.

[46] Edinburgh University Library, Gen. 284, Marjory Kennedy-Fraser, 'The Kennedys: A Life of Song', manuscript draft.

'The Road to the Isles'.[47] He later followed it up with a Gaelic version, but both the title and the idea of the song were original and '[t]here was no Gaelic model' behind Kenneth Macleod's composition.[48] It seems likely that she felt the Scots should have a song of their own – in a nationalistic sense – but apart from that and from performing at charity events, Kennedy-Fraser was never much involved in the war effort. On a private level, though, she was most certainly very worried as a mother, both when her son David was serving in France and when her daughter toured there as a field artiste with Lena Ashwell's 'Concerts at the Front'.

As Kennedy-Fraser's work became better known she gradually became officially recognized and she was awarded a state pension, followed by a CBE in 1924, and an Honorary Doctorate of Music from the University of Edinburgh in 1928. Her autobiography, *A Life of Song*, was published by Oxford University Press in 1929. Long sold out, a facsimile edition came out in 2011 from the Islands Book Trust, for which I had the great pleasure of supplying a comprehensive introduction. When she died in 1930, she was given a state funeral in Edinburgh's St Giles' Cathedral. Two years later, in July 1932, her ashes were interred in the precincts of the ancient cathedral on the island of Iona. A stone slab with a Celtic knot, designed by John Duncan, still marks the spot.

Both the *Songs of the Hebrides* and many of Kennedy-Fraser's other song arrangements and piano pieces remained popular and were regularly performed throughout the 1930s, but with changes in taste and preference, in particular during and after the Second World War, they gradually began to sink into oblivion and slowly vanished from the recital programmes. Some of her songs, though, having found their way into school song collections, lived on for many more years, albeit in much simplified and rather uninspired arrangements.

In the mid-twentieth century, art song recitals became a target for criticism of so-called 'high culture'. Large chunks of the repertoire were relegated to the attics. Scottish intellectuals voiced a strong aversion to what had come out of the Celtic Revival, despising what

---

[47] Kennedy-Fraser and Macleod, *Songs of the Hebrides* (1917), pp. 240–41: 'The Road to the Isles'/'A Tramping Song', words by Kenneth Macleod, to an air played by Malcolm Johnson, Barra, on the chanter, arranged for voice and harp (or piano) by Patuffa Kennedy-Fraser. Marjory Kennedy-Fraser's telling of how the song came about agrees with that of Kenneth Macleod's old friend Angus J. MacVicar. See Glasgow University Library, MS 1650, Box 61, 'The Road to the Isles', letter to the editor, *Oban Times*, 18 August 1962.
[48] Kennedy-Fraser, *A Life of Song*, pp. 150–51.

they considered a glorification of an invented fairy-tale past. The Scottish author Sorley MacLean was particularly scornful in his comments on the Kennedy-Frasers, as in an unpublished quatrain transcribed in the late 1930s by George Campbell Hay:

Soraidh le Nic Ualraig-Friseal,
bean uasal ise gun chron;
spoth i ar Ceòlraidh lùthmhor
's chuir i siùcair air an lot.

Farewell to Kennedy-Fraser,
an untarnished gentlewoman;
she gelded our vigorous Muses
and put sugar on the wound.[49]

In 1940, George Campbell Hay praised Sorley MacLean for not having 'wandered off into a drawingroom Tìr Nan Òg at the heels of the Clàrsach Society and the Kennedy Frasers'.[50] Equally venomous were the attacks on Kenneth Macleod.

The pendulum has swung once more, however, and many half-forgotten compositions from the late nineteenth and early twentieth centuries are now appearing regularly both on recordings and in recitals. A number of commercial Kennedy-Fraser recordings by distinguished performers are available.[51] Attitudes are also changing: 'One of the great delights of Gaelic song is the way in which the traditional material can be used in many forms from solo singing to rock music to orchestral arrangements', wrote Scottish musicologist Christopher MacLeod in 2002.[52] In 1930, Professor Tovey had written that 'the work [. . .] will surely be continued as to the use of these Hebridean songs by concert singers'.[53] Marjory Kennedy-Fraser's consummate recital versions undoubtedly merit their permanent place alongside the many well-known contributions of her contemporaries

---

[49] Somhairle MacGill-Eain/Sorley MacLean, *Dàin do Eimhir*, ed. Christopher Whyte (Glasgow: Association for Scottish Literary Studies, 2002), pp. 159–60 (English translation by Christopher Whyte).

[50] George Campbell Hay, *Collected Poems and Songs of George Campbell Hay (Deòrsa Mac Iain Dheòrsa)*, ed. Michel Byrne (Edinburgh: Edinburgh University Press, 2003), p. 503.

[51] *Land of Heart's Desire: Songs of the Hebrides from the Collection by Marjory Kennedy-Fraser*, Lisa Milne, soprano, and Sioned Williams, harp (Hyperion Records CDA66988, 1997); *Songs of Scotland*, Marie McLaughlin, soprano, Malcolm Martineau, piano, and Isobel Frayling-Cork, clarsach (Hyperion Records CDA67106, 2000).

[52] MacLeod, *Gaelic Music of the Hebrides*, p. 77.

[53] Tovey, 'An Appreciation'.

in the recitalists' standard art song repertoire, thereby giving presence to Gaelic Scotland in its rich chorus of Late Romantic voices from all corners of Europe and beyond.

Staged Authenticity in Folk Song Performance

SUE ALLAN

According to cultural historian Peter Burke, the humanities, including historical studies, over the past twenty years or so have taken a 'performative turn'.[1] Burke regards the trend as a development from earlier ideas of society as theatre, where culture is regarded as 'performance', from which developed the concept of 'occasionalism', whereby in different situations (in the presence of different people) a person behaves in different ways. For folklorists and musicologists, he suggests, this represents a shift of emphasis 'from texts to communicative events, their context and their reception', entailing a reframing of the folk song performance in the light of the event and its locale and audience.[2] Folk song scholarship has indeed turned to looking at the social context of songs and singers in recent years, and Steve Roud urges us to consider that it is not the origin of a song that makes it a folk song but rather its transmission within the folk tradition, despite which there has been relatively little study of song performance *per se*.[3] Drawing in part on my recent doctoral research into folk songs in Cumbria, this paper considers some of the questions raised in a study of folk song performance in various contexts.

The collectors of the first folk song revival undoubtedly put more emphasis on the song than the singer, while the performance context itself was often a personal visit or performance specially organized by their friends and correspondents. Scholars of the later twentieth century such as Dave Harker and Georgina Boyes have argued that the Victorian and Edwardian collectors systematically misrepresented the culture of working people, while pretending to champion it.[4] The

---

[1] Peter Burke, 'Performing History: The Importance of Occasions', *Rethinking History: The Journal of Theory and Practice*, 9 (2005), 35–52.

[2] Burke, 'Performing History', p. 38.

[3] Steve Roud, *Folk Song in England*, with music chapters by Julia Bishop (London: Faber & Faber, 2017), p. 24.

[4] Dave Harker, *Fakesong: The Manufacture of British 'Folksong', 1700 to the Present Day* (Milton Keynes: Open University Press, 1985); Georgina Boyes, *The Imagined Village:*

middle-class collectors of the first revival were framed as 'ideologically inspired mediators', appropriating cultural artefacts belonging to another class, with singers treated as 'repositories of songs' or conduits through whom folk song flowed, but who could otherwise be ignored.[5] These revisionist critiques did, however, highlight some important issues, notably the observation that the emotional appeal of the English folk revival encompassed the familiar themes of Romanticism: the cultural and spiritual superiority of the rural, and a celebration of the 'spontaneous simplicity' of folk song as opposed to the sophistication of art music.[6]

I would argue, however, that the accusation of middle-class expropriation does not stand up in every instance, as many English source singers, including Joseph Taylor (1833–1910), Henry Burstow (1826–1916), and John England (1865–1940), already enjoyed considerable status as performers within their own communities, sometimes even rewarded with drink or money. As part of this turn towards contextualization in folk music, with its renewed focus on singers, context, and process, the work of scholars such as Vic Gammon, Michael Pickering, David Atkinson, and Ian Russell, along with Richard Bauman's work on performance studies, has been invaluable, all of them enriching our understanding of folk song performance and giving new regionally based studies a firm theoretical grounding.

The event of performance: the Cumbrian context

Richard Bauman defines performance as 'a mode of communicative behaviour and a type of communicative event', and a music performance specifically as 'an aesthetically marked and heightened mode of communication, framed in a special way and put on display for an audience'.[7] What we might call the 'event of performance' in a folk song context includes a singer, a song, a time, and a place. Performance is 'situated, enacted, and rendered meaningful within socially defined situational contexts'; it is 'spatially bounded' and

---

Culture, Ideology and the English Folk Revival (Manchester: Manchester University Press, 1993).

[5] David Atkinson, 'Revival: Genuine or Spurious?', in *Folk Song: Tradition, Revival, and Re-Creation*, ed. Ian Russell and David Atkinson (Aberdeen: Elphinstone Institute, University of Aberdeen, 2004), pp. 144–62 (p. 145).

[6] Boyes, *Imagined Village*, p. 7.

[7] Richard Bauman, 'Performance', in *Folklore, Cultural Performances, and Popular Entertainments: A Communications-Centered Handbook*, ed. Richard Bauman (New York: Oxford University Press, 1992), 41–49 (p. 41).

'temporally bounded' (having a defined beginning and end), involves an audience, and also requires an occasioning principle such as a festival, concert, pub sing-song, recording, or meeting with a folk song collector.[8]

In contrast to the early collectors' framing of singers as mere conduits for songs, Roger Elbourne writes that folk performers actually sing with 'marked individuality', their choice of songs and style of singing both a reflection of their own taste and also of what they judge suitable for a specific performance context and audience.[9] In Cumbria,[10] the Kirkby Stephen blacksmith John Collinson (1861–1935), who sang for Frank Kidson and Cecil Sharp at the Westmorland Festival Folk Song Competitions of 1904–06, and the tweed salesman and pest control officer Micky Moscrop (1897–1997) of Carlisle, arguably the best performer on the 1953 archive recordings later issued commercially as *Pass the Jug Round*, were both well-regarded, accomplished performers in their own localities. Singers may exhibit varying degrees of skill, talent, taste, and imagination, but those like Collinson and Moscrop are conscious of audience appeal, take pride in their performance, and practise to perfect their art.

The performance event in his or her own community is the traditional singer's personal showcase and also functions as an affirmation of group identity: 'the occasion and event which fosters through social interaction and participation the collective consciousness and affirmation of group identity [and] a driving, crystallizing force in the enacting display of a given social group's aesthetics, that is, the value systems that validate the group's ethos.'[11] This is very much the case with hunt and shepherds' meets. In my thesis on folk song in Cumbria I made an attempt to identify the contexts in which folk songs were performed by classifying performance settings as informal, semi-formal, or formal:

---

[8] Bauman, 'Performance', pp. 45–46.

[9] Roger Elbourne, *Music and Tradition in Early Industrial Lancashire, 1780–1840* (Woodbridge: D. S. Brewer; Totowa, NJ: Rowman and Littlefield, for the Folklore Society, 1980), p. 104.

[10] The county name Cumbria is used here as a convenient shorthand – despite its appearing anachronistic because it dates back only to 1974, when the historic counties of Cumberland and Westmorland, with Lancashire North of the Sands and a corner of the Yorkshire Dales, were merged – as most historical studies acknowledge that because of its geography the area has considerable cultural and social coherence.

[11] Gerard Henri Béhague, 'Music Performance', in *Folklore, Cultural Performances, and Popular Entertainments: A Communications-Centred Handbook*, ed. Richard Bauman (New York: Oxford University Press, 1992), pp. 172–77 (p. 176).

Informal: the home (most often where women sang), the public house, fairs and markets where ballad singers/sellers performed

Semi-formal: rural 'merry neets', urban harmonic societies, work-related events such as harvest ('kurn') suppers, sheep shearings ('boon clippings'), and shepherds' meets, as well as hunt suppers – all events where a chairman is elected to take charge of proceedings for the evening

Formal: church, theatre, concert hall, and formal dinners like those organized for Lakeland Dialect Society competitions, as well as folk song competitions, performance for folk song collectors, audio recordings and broadcasts, and folk clubs and festivals.[12]

While this proved useful in order to group together particular types of songs sung on different occasions and to map the various singers on to those events, I am unsure about how useful such a categorization might be in a wider context. Some of the insights gained from the exercise did prove quite illuminating, however, particularly regarding singers' performances for folk song collectors who were seeking 'authenticity' and 'tradition'. However, as Dan Ben-Amos notes, the idea of tradition has 'accumulated a patina of meanings with its own luster',[13] and today we might also characterize it as hiding an accumulation of ambiguities. Although the concept of tradition is sometimes placed in opposition to performance – the first being static and in the past, the second dynamically in the present – Ben-Amos suggests they should be considered as complementary. He also offers a useful comparison with Ferdinand de Saussure's conceptual model of *langue* and *parole*: thus *langue*, which describes the normative rules of language or behaviour in a given situation, equates with tradition, while *parole*, which represents an individual's choice and use of the rules, is evidenced in a performance.[14]

Performances for folk song collectors

Many country singers sought out by the Victorian and Edwardian folk song collectors were far from being 'untainted primitive[s] without any real creative agency or access to the tools of critical enquiry

---

[12] Sue Allan, 'Folk Song in Cumbria: A Distinctive Regional Repertoire?' (unpublished doctoral thesis, Lancaster University, 2017), 179.

[13] Dan Ben-Amos, 'The Seven Strands of Tradition: Varieties in its Meaning in American Folklore Studies', *Journal of Folklore Research*, 21 (1984), 97–131 (p. 124).

[14] Ben-Amos, 'Seven Strands of Tradition', pp. 121–22.

provided by literacy',[15] but were often accomplished and experienced singers of a variety of types of music, who performed in a range of venues, including churches and concert halls. John England of Hambridge in Somerset, for example, from whom Cecil Sharp famously collected his first folk song, 'The Seeds of Love', was also sexton of his parish church and sang in the choir and at choir socials, so may well have been able to read music.[16] Henry Burstow of Horsham, Sussex, provided Lucy Broadwood with many folk songs, but his vast repertoire consisted of a diverse range of songs and he was also an accomplished bell-ringer.[17]

Joseph Taylor in Lincolnshire, from whom Percy Grainger noted 'Brigg Fair', also sang in his church choir, as well as at the music festival where Grainger first heard him, and had always had a keen interest in music. His granddaughter relates that he even called his dog Minim, because it had one spot on its back, saying, 'he couldn't be a crotchet, he has no stick, and anyhow he must have a musical name'.[18] That Taylor was musically self-aware was acknowledged by Grainger, albeit somewhat condescendingly: 'He most intelligently realizes just what sort of songs collectors are after, distinguishes surprisingly between genuine traditional tunes and other ditties, and is, in every way, a marvel of helpfulness and kindliness.'[19]

Likewise, in Cumbria we find singers with wide and diverse repertoires choosing to sing only certain songs in particular contexts: 'folk songs' if they were requested, dialect songs at appropriate gatherings, hunting songs or songs on farming themes at hunt and shepherds' meets, and so on. An example is John Collinson who, after winning the Kendal Folk Song Competition in 1905, was subsequently visited by both Percy Grainger and Anne Gilchrist, who also collected from two other singers in the Kirkby Lonsdale area, carpenter James

---

[15] Graham Freeman, "'It wants all the creases ironing out": Percy Grainger, the Folk Song Society, and the Ideology of the Archive', *Music & Letters*, 92 (2011), 410–36 (p. 416).

[16] Derek Schofield, 'Sowing the Seeds: Cecil Sharp and Charles Marson in Somerset', *Folk Music Journal*, 8.4 (2004), 484–512 (pp. 492–93); Stephen Banfield, *Music in the West Country: Social and Cultural History across an English Region* (Woodbridge: Boydell Press, 2018), pp. 265–66.

[17] Vic Gammon, "'Not Appreciated in Worthing?' Class Expression and Popular Song Texts in Mid-Nineteenth-Century Britain', *Popular Music*, 4 (1984), 5–24.

[18] E. Marion Hudson, *Brigg Fair: A Memoir of Joseph Taylor by his Grand-daughter*, ed. Peter Collinson (2003), [pp. 6, 17] https://www.family-trees.org.uk/histories/history_templates/brigg_fair_history_template.php.

[19] Hudson, *Brigg Fair*, [p. 26].

Bayliff and Mrs Carlisle.[20] Collinson was just forty-seven and Gilchrist described him as a man 'with a fine ear for a song', who had 'some education', as well as a keen competitive streak.[21] She made the same general point about all her singers from the Kirkby Lonsdale area: 'The singers were not illiterate, like many in Southern England whose ballads have been taken down; a rather higher degree of literacy would have ranked them with the makers of some of the ballads they sang.'[22] According to his grandson, Collinson was also an aspiring writer of poetry, writing songs, poems, and articles for local publication, and had a keen idea of his own worth as a performer.[23] This apparent contradiction, which sees folk singers as self-aware performers, tuning their repertoires and performances to the demands of their audiences, but also as naive, uneducated purveyors of 'authentic' folk music, merits further examination.

Authenticity and staged authenticity

The quest for authenticity began in the eighteenth century and came to fruition in the full flowering of Romanticism in the early nineteenth century, as has been very well documented by Matthew Gelbart.[24] It was this same Romanticism that underpinned the first folk revival and its conception of real folk music as performed by a rural peasantry, heirs to ancient songs and airs. It is, however, also possible to frame the revival as an 'invented tradition', which, as articulated by Eric Hobsbawm, is something that offers a sense of continuity with a historic past.[25] Although the very appearance of movements for the defence or revival of traditions might be seen as indicative of a break with the past (since where the old ways are alive, traditions need be neither revived nor invented), Hobsbawm draws a distinction between 'tradition' and 'custom': the first characteristically comprising fixed and formalized practices, while the second does not preclude

---

[20] VWML, Anne Geddes Gilchrist Collection, transcriptions of songs from Westmorland singers (see AGG/3, AGG/5, AGG/8).

[21] Anne Gilchrist, 'Some Old Westmorland Folk-Singers', *Journal of the Lakeland Dialect Society*, no. 4 (November 1942), pp. 5–14 (p. 8).

[22] Gilchrist, 'Some Old Westmorland Folk-Singers', p. 5.

[23] John Collinson's grandson John, interview with Sue Allan, Kirkby Lonsdale, 1 October 2013.

[24] Matthew Gelbart, *The Invention of 'Folk Music' and 'Art Music': Emerging Categories from Ossian to Wagner* (Cambridge: Cambridge University Press, 2007).

[25] Eric Hobsbawm, 'Introduction: Inventing Traditions', in *The Invention of Tradition*, ed. Eric Hobsbawm and Terence Ranger (Cambridge: Cambridge University Press, 1983), pp. 1–14.

innovation and change, up to a point. The same might be said of folk song, where evolution and change, along with a degree of artistic innovation, reflect a much more complex relationship between continuity and evolution, tradition and change.

Questions of authenticity and the invention of tradition frequently become entwined in debates about the nature of folk music and are often expressed as polar opposites. A more nuanced view might be to accept that pure invention is rare because its building blocks are generally taken from something that has gone before. Just as singers' interpretations of songs develop over time, songs evolve and traditions are reshaped. Authenticity is a loaded term, which has been described as a relative concept, generally used in absolutist terms but actually a matter of interpretation, something that is 'ascribed, not inscribed' – ascribed to a performance by an observer and therefore 'a construction made on the act of listening'.[26] But authenticity can also be ascribed by the singer him- or herself, in the belief that they are 'performing authenticity'.

If the invention of tradition seems at first sight to be something of an oxymoron, then the concept of 'staged authenticity' appears even more so, but I believe it may prove a useful model for a study of folk song performance. The term was coined by the sociologist Dean MacCannell, who argued that tourism can usefully be framed as a modern reinterpretation of pilgrimage, where tourists seek out the 'sacred', which in this context resides in the seemingly authentic local customs, songs, or dances presented to them in tourist locales.[27] Referencing Erving Goffman's dramaturgical approach to social interaction,[28] staged authenticity, according to MacCannell, comprises performers, audience, and others situated in the taken-for-granted reality of a social performance, which in fact depends on structural arrangements such as the concealment of the stage-management of a performance.

Staged authenticity in Cumbria

The turn to contextualization in folk song scholarship brought with it an increased focus on the local and the particular, bringing new

---

[26] Allan Moore, 'Authenticity as Authentication', *Popular Music*, 21 (2002), 209–23 (p. 210).

[27] Dean MacCannell, 'Staged Authenticity: Arrangements of Social Space in Tourist Settings', *American Journal of Sociology*, 79 (1973), 590–603.

[28] Erving Goffman, *The Presentation of Self in Everyday Life* (New York: Doubleday, 1959), pp. 144–45.

insights into both repertoire and performance. Elbourne's study of industrial Lancashire, for example, reveals a musical life in both the pre-industrial weaving communities and the industrial towns of the region 'far more rich, varied and complex than has been generally assumed', with pre-industrial, rural forms of folk song persisting in industrial areas giving rise to the emergence of what he calls a 'hybrid musical activity'.[29] Cumbrians similarly exercised their musical talents in a range of different contexts: at home, in concerts, at soirées linked to churches, as well as in public houses, where those known to be performers would be called upon to entertain and, where appropriate, lend their support to the cause.[30] A communal event in any town or village would have been inconceivable without music, with the songs chosen being those most suitable for the particular context.

In the nineteenth and early twentieth centuries, many events might have included songs by Carlisle dialect poet Robert Anderson (1770–1833), who, in both his life and work, embodied the apparently contradictory elements of urban and rural, printed and oral transmission, and traditional as well as commercial music. Many of his dialect songs went into the repertoire of local singers down the years and came to be regarded as authentic folk songs, rooted in the local community and performed by generations of singers. Yet they were also products of the revival of dialect in literary form which began in Cumbria in the eighteenth century and reached its zenith in Cumbria, Lancashire, and Yorkshire in the middle of the nineteenth century. Anderson's dialect is, though, fairly lightly inflected, as he intended his work to be bought, read, and sung by as many people as possible. In that light, he could be said to be 'performing dialect' in a similar way to Robert Burns, whose language, it has been claimed, represents a form of 'stage Scots' easily accessible to a wider audience.[31]

Other 'performances of authenticity' in Cumbria might include the very large joint hunt and shepherds' meets held at Mardale in the eastern Lake District (the village now under the waters of Haweswater reservoir). In the nineteenth and early twentieth centuries, meets were attended not only by local huntsmen, shepherds, farmers, and villagers, but by a wide variety of middle-class hunt supporters and hunting song aficionados/writers from across the north of England.[32]

---

[29] Elbourne, *Music and Tradition in Early Industrial Lancashire*, p. 3.

[30] Lyn Murfin, *Popular Leisure in the Lake Counties* (Manchester: Manchester University Press, 1990), p. 175.

[31] Alex Broadhead, 'A Sprinkling of Stage Scots: Burns, Linguistic Stereotypes and Place', *Scottish Literary Review*, 3 (2011), 21–42 (pp. 26–27).

[32] *Cumberland & Westmorland Herald*, 29 November 1924, p. 7.

Another example might be the regular meetings of expatriate Cumbrians living and working in London, like the Cumberland Free and Easy reported on in the Carlisle journal *The Citizen* in 1829.[33] Attended by all classes of people, the songs included Anderson's 'Barbary Bell', 'The Buck o' Kingwatter', and 'Sweet Sally Gray', albeit sung by a 'not altogether sober company [. . .] a combination of sounds most discordant'.

From around 1867 onwards, we find William Metcalfe (1830–1909), composer, singer, and conductor of the Carlisle Choral Society, arranging dialect songs by Anderson and others for performance on the concert platform and publishing his arrangements in sheet music form. Later, in the 1920s, Carlisle-born Jeffrey Mark (1898–1965) arranged a series of dialect songs for performance by a male voice choir in Carlisle. Mark, a classically trained professor of composition at the Royal College of Music, had also played in informal village bands from the age of ten and retained his early contact with traditional musicians in the area, evidently happy to move freely between different musical genres and circles of performers.[34] He published and performed his settings of traditional airs for Cumberland dialect songs with the specific object of stimulating interest in local folk songs, and his 1927 concert proved so successful that it was repeated at Keswick, Cockermouth, and Penrith, and some of his arrangements were later broadcast.[35]

The influence of both Metcalfe and Mark was long-lasting. In 1905, Metcalfe's versions of Anderson's ballads were sung by choral society members Mr Henderson, James Walter Brown, and John Carruthers for Sydney Nicholson (1875–1947), acting organist of Carlisle Cathedral, who then sent his transcriptions to Lucy Broadwood. A selection was published in the *Journal of the Folk-Song Society* the following year, and some were also transcribed from Mr Carruthers by Ralph Vaughan Williams when he visited Carlisle in 1906.[36] Fifty years later, Carlisle entertainer Joe Wallace broadcast

---

[33] K. I., 'Cumberland Free and Easy in London', *The Citizen*, no. 11 (1 May 1829), pp. 289–92. The venue was the Crown and Sugarloaf in Fleet Street.

[34] Jeffrey Mark, 'Recollections of Folk-Musicians', *Music Quarterly*, 16 (1930), 170–85.

[35] Norman Nicholson, 'City Concert Launched a Folk Music Revival', *Cumberland News*, 12 June 1987, p. 4.

[36] VWML, Lucy Broadwood Manuscript Collection, LEB/5/350, LEB/5/351; London, British Library, Add. MS 71700 f.0., letter from Ralph Vaughan Williams to Ralph Wedgwood; London, British Library, Add. MS 54191, Ralph Vaughan Williams MSS, vol. 3, book 11 (VWML, RVW2/3/229–RVW2/3/235); *Journal of the Folk-Song Society*, no. 3.1 (no. 10) (1907), 39–46.

some of Mark's and Metcalfe's dialect song arrangements on the BBC's Northern Service's *Merry Neet* and *Barn Dance* programmes, which also featured another notable local singer and musician, Robert Forrester. All the performers were paid by the BBC, with Forrester getting five or six guineas per programme and Wallace paid nine or ten guineas plus travelling expenses.[37]

Bob Forrester (1913–88) is better known for his participation in the archive recordings made in 1953 at the village pubs in Rockcliffe and Wreay, near Carlisle. He was, in fact, one of the instigators of the recording project, along with his friend and colleague Norman Alford and Carlisle archivist Tom Gray. Many of the original recordings were released as a commercial LP, *Pass the Jug Round*, in 1982, and on CD in 2002.[38] It is clear from the recordings that quite a number of the singers, particularly Bob Forrester and Micky Moscrop, are self-aware and self-assured performers, keen to assert their Cumbrian identity both in their introductions and in their choice of songs – mainly hunting songs and songs in dialect. Recordings and broadcasts always, of course, entail organization and some direction, and here it is notable that the singers use a much more strongly inflected dialect when introducing themselves and their songs than they do when singing. Joe Thompson's remark, 'Will that dee for ye?' ('Will that do for you?'), at the end of his introduction reveals the stage-management of the occasion.

Shortly before the release of *Pass the Jug Round* in 1982, Bob Forrester was interviewed on BBC Radio Cumbria, an interview notable not for the rich north Cumbrian dialect he used in 1953, but for his everyday language – standard English with a slight northern accent. Describing the musical history of his family, he said: 'My grandfather I never knew, as he died before I was born, but my father inherited tunes and songs from my grandfather, who was a great fiddler in the Bewcastle area.'[39] This was markedly different from the way he expressed himself on the 1953 recordings: 'Ma naame is Robert Forrester an' ah was born in Cummerlan'. The Border waltz which me friend Norman Alford an' me are goin' to plaay has come doon ta me with the fiddle me gran'faither used to play it on.' Although he and Alford were indeed both Carlisle lads with a love of

---

[37] Caversham, BBC Written Records Archive, N18/3899, BBC Artist File: Joe Wallace; N18/1215/1, BBC Artist File: Robert (Bob) Forrester; Robert Forrester, letter to Sue Allan, 9 April 1982.

[38] Carlisle Archive Centre, acetate recordings DX938/1 (1953); *Pass the Jug Round*, LP (Reynard Records RR002, 1982); *Pass the Jug Round*, CD (Veteran VT142CD, 2002).

[39] Robert Forrester, interviewed by Irene Mallis, BBC Radio Cumbria, 4 June 1980.

local songs, and the recordings were the fruit of their many visits to country pubs over the years, the two friends were far from being the unsophisticated purveyors of a music tradition they had 'inherited'. Both were trained graphic designers, with a keen interest in local history, and were active members of the Lakeland Dialect Society. Forrester's code-switching between Cumberland dialect and standard English provides evidence that he changed his usage when required: standard English for a radio interview, but the dialect of the 1953 recordings to provide 'audible proof' of his being authentically Cumbrian.[40]

There does not seem to be any suggestion that any of the Cumbrian concerts, broadcasts, or recordings were considered by the public as in any way 'inauthentic'. We too easily dismiss Victorian and Edwardian concert arrangements of folk songs while accepting contemporary folk performers' innovative arrangements. In fact, the conventions of art music and folk music have long been intertwined, with categories of classical and folk, traditional and commercial, or amateur and professional happily jumbled and freely interchangeable. Thus we have source singers who were also collectors: John Collinson and Bob Forrester, for example. Jeffrey Mark, a professional classical composer, was originally a folk musician. And well before Cecil Sharp and his contemporaries were arranging folk songs for the concert platform we find William Metcalfe arranging Cumbrian dialect songs for concert performance by members of Carlisle Choral Society, some of them later transcribed by Vaughan Williams as folk songs.[41] Keen amateur performers like Micky Moscrop, who sang with a concert party in the 1920s, appear to have been just as happy singing on stage as in the pub, or even, like Joe Wallace and Bob Forrester, at a BBC microphone. Which then is the 'authentic' voice of the people?

One factor common to all of these performances by Cumbrian singers, whether at a traditional Cumberland 'merry neet', at a seasonal event like a shepherds' meet or hunt supper, or in a more formal performance setting, is that they were keen to express their local identity, their Cumbrian distinctiveness. We need to be aware, though, that such expressions of regional identity might also represent a form of staged authenticity. Not all the singers on the *Pass the Jug Round* recordings, for example, were members of the hunting and farming

---

[40] Cf. Taryn Hakala, 'A Great Man in Clogs: Performing Authenticity in Victorian Lancashire', *Victorian Studies*, 52 (2010), 387–412 (p. 395).

[41] James Walter Brown, *Round Carlisle Cross* (Carlisle: Thurnams, 1950), pp. 206–11; Carlisle, Jackson Library, D52, The Works of William Metcalfe, vol. 2.

communities traditionally associated with those songs, but instead worked in very different milieux. Tom Brodie was a water-bailiff working for the river authority; Harvey Nicholson was a railway plate-layer; Micky Moscrop was employed in the widely disparate roles of tweed salesman and pest control officer. These singers, along with the initiators of the recording project, Bob Forrester and Norman Alford, appear quite consciously to have been 'performing regional identity', in songs like Forrester's 'Corby Castle' ('Wetheral Green') or 'Copshawholme Fair', as well as in their introductions. However, for Joe Thompson, who sang 'Joe Bowman', 'The Horn of the Hunter', and 'The Welton Hunt', his motivation was clearly a love of hunting. As for Micky Moscrop ('John Peel' and 'Pass the Jug Round'), he appears to have sung for the sheer delight of performing for an audience. It seems that singers, even on the same occasion, do not necessarily share a common experience or ascribe the same meaning to their performances. What they do share is simply their participation in a particular performance context, singing a repertoire of songs which they, and their audience, invest with a diverse range of meanings.

The chimera of authenticity

It seems then that 'authentic' folk song performance may be just a chimera, given that singers do not necessarily perform naively or unreflectively. In fact, according to Jeff Todd Titon, most 'can and do discuss and evaluate aspects of performance and repertoire among themselves'.[42] Such a validation of community is part and parcel of what I call 'performing regional identity', which became a major element of mid-twentieth-century folk song performance in Cumbria and other English regions. Later twentieth-century Cumbrian folk performers, like Wesley Park, Stuart Lawrence, Paul and Linda Adams, Angie Marchant, and myself, were similarly keen to assert local identity and promote it to a wider audience.

Do such performances of regional identity fall into the category of staged authenticity? Perhaps so, although the term in its original conception referred to a presentation for tourists, whereas very often with Cumbrian dialect and hunting songs the performances are aimed primarily at local people. The meaning of a performance is not entirely inscribed in its context, or its framing and stage-management, but is

---

[42] Jeff Todd Titon, 'Music, Folk and Tradition', in *Folklore, Cultural Performances, and Popular Entertainments: A Communications-Centred Handbook* (New York: Oxford University Press, 1992), pp. 167–71 (pp. 168–69).

actually a different experience for every performer and for every member of the audience. Yet song as a form of communication does seem able to renew and strengthen group identity, reinforcing the coherence of groups, even if the songs themselves are capable of being invested with a diverse range of meanings, including authenticity, by the singers themselves.[43]

The common thread running throughout our wonderfully muddled categories of performers and performance contexts is the willingness of singers who delight in presenting their songs in a wide range of venues, from local pub to concert stage and even the BBC. They may often quite consciously be 'performing regional identity', and taking pleasure in doing so, but that may not always be the case. We too easily fall into the trap of treating 'local' folk song as if it were a completely unified, defined form channelling the past, whereas the local exists in the national (and vice versa), just as the past exists in the present, and people live, love, work, play, and sing in a range of different contexts.[44] We do well to remember David Atkinson's words, that the relationship between the past and the present 'is both continuous and discontinuous, or both real and imaginary',[45] and to keep in mind that 'histories are also fictions – something made of the past', which we know in a double way, since we read or hear them in the present.[46]

As Gelbart warns, if we dismiss the idea of authenticity entirely, 'we run the risk of overlooking the power that the concept has had on the very sources we use to look at this material', as the concepts of authenticity and tradition have been integral to our understanding of the history of folk music and what people have believed about it – for both folk music scholars and performers, 'perception has formed its own reality.'[47] Both authenticity and invention are involved in a tradition that evolves and is reshaped over time, with even staged authenticity being seen as historically perfectly valid. We also need to keep in mind that our 'source singers', who sang their old and not so old, local and not so local, songs for us all to enjoy and perhaps perform again, were not one-dimensional but rather people who

---

[43] Deborah Kermode, *The Shepherd's Voice: Song and Upland Shepherds of 19th and Early 20th Century Lakeland* (unpublished master's dissertation, Lancaster University, 2003), p. 51.

[44] Ana Maria Alonso, 'The Effects of Truth: Re-Presentations of the Past and the Imagining of Community', *Journal of Historical Sociology*, 1 (1988), 33–57 (p. 47).

[45] Atkinson, 'Revival: Genuine or Spurious?', p. 148.

[46] Greg Dening, *Performances* (Chicago: Chicago University Press, 1996), p. 37.

[47] Gelbart, *Invention of 'Folk Music' and 'Art Music'*, p. 274.

fulfilled many different roles in life – workers, lovers, parents, children, Cumbrians, and performers of their own perception of reality, authentically.

Patience Vaisey: A Woman's Repertoire in 1892

BOB ASKEW

Patience Vaisey at Adwell, 1892 is a CD of Patience Vaisey's full noted repertoire of sixteen songs, sung by three contemporary singers: Annie Winter, Alison Frosdick, and Anna Baldwin. There is no known sound recording of Patience Vaisey and the three singers provide three different takes on what she might have sounded like and how she might have treated the songs. I researched the material and produced the CD, which was recorded by John Dipper. 'The Banks of Sweet Primroses' (sung by Anna Baldwin on the CD) was Patience Vaisey's 'greatest hit', because it is the version that everyone learned from *The Penguin Book of English Folk Songs.*[1] Apart from 'My Bonny Bonny Boy', however, the rest of her repertoire seems to have been forgotten. The songs were noted by Lucy Broadwood in 1892, right at the beginning of effective English folk song collecting, and I believe it is an important collection.

Women are under-represented in all the great collections, and we are still doing it today. It remains difficult to pick out the token women among the mass of male performers in folk festival programmes, and it is probably the same in folk clubs and arts centres. I decided to produce the CD of Patience's songs in order to redress the balance a fraction. I will first describe Patience's family background – her childhood and her life working as a servant and then married to a gardener – and then examine her songs.

Patience Vaisey and her family

There is no surviving relative to pass on Patience's story, so I have had to reconstruct her life from census, birth, marriage, and death records, and a short note by Lucy Broadwood. She was born Patience Cooper in 1848 in Sherborne St John, a small village a few miles north

---

[1] Ralph Vaughan Williams and A. L. Lloyd (eds), *The Penguin Book of English Folk Songs* (Harmondsworth: Penguin, 1959), p. 15; reissued as *Classic English Folk Songs*, ed. Malcolm Douglas (London: EFDSS, 2003), with 'The Banks of Sweet Primroses' on p. 5, but mistakenly noted as from Hertfordshire rather than Hampshire The editor apologized profusely for this error.

of Basingstoke, Hampshire. Her father, an agricultural worker, died just before she was born. Her mother must have struggled to provide for his two children, as well as two daughters from a previous marriage. She was noted as a 'pauper' in the census of 1851, suggesting she was in receipt of benefit.

Patience's mother was also named Patience Cooper. Her two husbands were older than her. This might explain why her daughter did not include the well-known 'Never Wed an Old Man' in her own repertoire, if it was a touchy subject at home. Her mother married for a third time in 1853. This was probably another marriage of convenience, because this time her husband was a much younger man.

Young Patience endured poverty as a child, and rural women were only paid half the wages that men received, so her prospects were not great. It is no wonder that she sought secure work as a servant, and she worked in service until she was aged thirty-one. Servants usually received their training at a young age in a house close to home. Once trained, however, employers often wanted servants from far away, because they did not want family ties interfering with their work, or for servants to have the security of a strong local social group.

The life of a servant was near-slavery to modern eyes, and it is no wonder that domestic service started to decline once people tasted better hours and wages in the First World War. Service did, however, provide clothing, shelter, and regular meals. This would probably have been attractive to Patience after her precarious childhood. By 1871 she was working at Busbridge Hall, Surrey, twenty-five miles from her home.[2] In those days this would have represented a total severance, because servants worked very long hours and had very little time off. They usually had one day off each month, and one week's holiday per year. Patience would have been able to visit her home village at most once a year. The broken-token songs, of which there were two in her repertoire, were popular in her day, and I believe this was because thousands of people were forced to work far from their homes and loved ones.

Did Patience continue to sing as a servant? It is difficult to know how much servants were permitted to sing. They were probably banned from singing in the house during their long working hours. In their scarce leisure time, however, they may have been permitted, and even encouraged, to sing. Employers liked to build up loyalty and social cohesion among their staff, who came from many different

---

[2] Busbridge Hall, Home Farm Road, Godalming, Surrey GU7 1XG, is a new building which replaced the Hall where Patience worked.

parts of the country. So Patience probably sang her songs to her fellow servants. Nearly all of them were young unmarried women, like herself, and her repertoire of love songs would have appealed to them. 'Oh Why Was I Born to be Tormented So', a rare Hampshire song, would have had a particular appeal because the prospects for love and marriage were very poor for servants.

Employers preferred their servants to be single, and if they struck up a relationship they were dismissed. Patience did marry, however, at the age of thirty-one. She was married in Cowley, a village to the north-west of London, now swallowed up by the city. She probably worked for the Hilliard family at Cowley House, and it was there that she met her husband, Richard Vaisey, a gardener from Wiltshire. They were married in 1880. Another of her songs was 'And a-Courting I Went When I'd Nothing Else To Do'.

Patience and Richard worked briefly in central London but soon moved to West Lodge Park, Enfield, just north of the city, where their two children were born. The house survives as a hotel run by the Beale family today, and Andrew Beale kindly gave us permission to use a picture of three servants serving a family picnic in the 1880s, when Patience was there.[3] We do not know if she is one of them, but she would certainly have known them.

The next census, in 1891, shows the Vaiseys at Adwell House in Oxfordshire, and it was there that Lucy Broadwood noted her songs in 1892, when she was visiting her cousin, Herbert Birch Reynardson.[4] The House still belongs to the Reynardson family, and Tom Birch Reynardson kindly gave permission to use two contemporary watercolours for the CD. One of them shows two gardeners just before the Vaiseys moved there, so Richard Vaisey probably looked very similar when he was working. The gardens look much the same today, although the round flowerbeds are now grassed over.

Patience and her family then moved on to Barnsley Park, Gloucestershire, where they were recorded in the 1901 census.[5] They finally settled, and Patience died there in 1923, at the age of seventy-four. So, after working all over southern England, they settled in Gloucestershire and neither she nor her husband returned to live in their home area.

---

[3] West Lodge Park Hotel, Cockfosters Road, Barnet EN4 0PY.

[4] Adwell House, Thame, Oxfordshire OX9 7DQ.

[5] Barnsley Park, Barnsley, Gloucestershire GL7 5EG.

Lucy Broadwood and the songs

Lucy Broadwood noted Patience's songs in 1892 and published six of them over the next twenty years in *English County Songs* (1893) and the *Journal of the Folk-Song Society*. She wrote of Patience in the 1904 *Journal*:

> When I expressed a hope that her children would learn them [her songs] she said, 'They like to pick them up from me, and I like the old ballads myself, but my husband he says, "Don't teach them that rubbish! Give them *Hymns Ancient and Modern!*"'[6]

So Richard Vaisey felt that all songs should be religious and, sadly, it appears that he did not appreciate his wife's traditional songs. This may well have discouraged Patience from learning more songs, and it may explain why her repertoire is limited to love songs from her youth and her unmarried life in service. Richard Vaisey did not impose a ban, however, because she did sing her songs to her children – and she must have been known as a singer for Lucy Broadwood to have heard about her. (See *Appendix* for a list of the songs collected by Broadwood.)

Patience's songs preserved at the Vaughan Williams Memorial Library have only the tunes in manuscript, the texts are not there. Lucy Broadwood published six songs with both texts and tunes, so it would seem that she noted the texts, but they have presumably been lost at some stage. The tunes, however, give the songs most of their individual character, and most were relatively easy to reconstruct using texts from singers from a similar geographical area. If no collected versions were available, they were reconstructed from broadsides. Once I had done this, I realized that it was an interesting and important collection and set out to organize the CD recordings.

A 'women's repertoire'?

I would like to suggest that women sang a wider range of songs than men and that Patience's repertoire is interesting because it highlights a narrower 'women's repertoire' of songs that men did not usually sing.

Alfred Williams wrote of the folk songs of the upper Thames: 'The women's songs were chiefly the sweetest of all [. . .] They were rarely sung by the males. The women might sing some of the men's pieces, but the men seldom sang those of women.'[7] I think 'most beautiful'

---

[6] *Journal of the Folk-Song Society*, 1.5 (1904), 267.

[7] Alfred Williams (ed.), *Folk-Songs of the Upper Thames* (London: Duckworth, 1923), p. 19.

might have been a better description, but otherwise there seem to be few comments by collectors about women's repertoires, so Alfred Williams's observations are important. They seem to indicate that women sang a selection of songs that men did not sing.

This is confusing for us today because it does not seem to accord with what other collectors noted. They seem to have taken down a lot of 'women's songs' (which I interpret as 'songs from the viewpoint of a woman') from men. This could be explained by men having learned women's songs by frequent hearing, when families or couples sang together. The collectors could then have persuaded the men to sing the women's songs when they asked for every traditional song that they knew. The collectors would merely have noted down the man's name as being the person who sang, so this could have left a false impression of men's and women's repertoires in the past. Or male singers singing women's songs might be a twentieth-century phenomenon, once they realized that collectors were interested in the women's songs, and also once modern songbooks came into the men's hands.

Fifteen years later, George Gardiner noted songs from other women of a similar age in Axford, a few miles south of Sherborne St John. They all had a much wider repertoire than Patience, which ties in with what Alfred Williams wrote about women singing the men's songs as well.

When I first heard all of Patience's songs together I found it a very beautiful repertoire, very varied in tone, consisting of songs relating to love in many different circumstances. Then, after reading Alfred Williams, I thought the repertoire might highlight these 'women's songs' because it does not include the wider range of songs that both men and women sang. This is a personal feeling and it would be difficult to adduce any proof. The majority of Patience's songs have, in fact, been noted more or less equally from both men and women.

The importance of the repertoire

Patience Vaisey's repertoire is important because it is one of the earliest repertoires collected from a woman. Half of her songs were popular throughout the nineteenth century and remained so during the heyday of English folk song collecting before the First World War. But even those are of interest because many of the tunes are different from the well-known versions. Lucy Broadwood wrote about the version of 'Barbara Allen' that 'it differs much from any usually found'.[8] She also noted that the 'Ploughing Song' shows traces of the Dorian mode.[9] 'I Courted a Bonny Lass; or, The False Lover', too, is different from the well-known tune. Two of Patience's songs, 'In Rochester City' and 'Oh Why Was I Born', are rare and have only been collected in Hampshire or occasionally in adjacent counties. To me, this underlines the idea that she learned them when she was young, before she left home.

Patience also had a number of songs that are important because they were popular in the mid-nineteenth century but rarely sung by c.1900. There were many broadside printings in the mid-century of 'The Garland of Love' and 'How Sweet in the Woodlands', for example, but both seem to have become very rare by the end of the century. These two items are also of interest because they could be classified as 'art songs', as the collectors called them, composed for the stage or the drawing room. This kind of song was popular with folk singers alongside the more traditional ones, but they were largely ignored by the collectors. So Patience's repertoire also gives a truer picture of the wider range of songs that traditional singers sang. Alison Fosdick found a published version of 'When the Moon Stands on Tiptoe', which may also have started as an art song. It was rarely noted, however, and was thought to be a traditional hunting song.

Two more songs seem to be lighter stage songs: 'Nothing Else to Do' and 'Among the Green Hay'. There were several broadside printings of the former and seven collected versions, but 'Among the Green Hay' seems to have been rarer, with only one surviving broadside and four collected versions. We are indebted to Martin Graebe for this song, which was lost from the Lucy Broadwood collection but found in Baring Gould's collection, where clearly both text and tune are from Patience Vaisey. It is one of the rare songs about 'love and spelling'.

Lucy Broadwood published only six out of sixteen of Patience's songs, so this is probably the first time that many of them have been sung for over a hundred years, and it must certainly be the first time that they have been all sung together in public in that time. The songs serve as a memorial to Patience and also, I think, to all the unknown singers of the past whose lives we can now only reconstruct from threadbare records. Women singers were infrequently collected, but many may have had a similar repertoire, and most, I believe, would

---

[8] *Journal of the Folk-Song Society*, 1.5 (1904), 267.
[9] London, Vaughan Williams Memorial Library, Lucy Broadwood Manuscript Collection, LEB/2/66/3.

have expanded it to contain a wider range that included songs sung by men. Patience Vaisey's collected repertoire highlights the women's songs and is attractive and interesting in its own right.

Appendix: Repertoire of Patience Vaisey as noted by Lucy Broadwood

LEB: VWML, Lucy Broadwood Manuscript Collection.
SBG: Sabine Baring-Gould manuscripts (via VWML Digital Archive).
JFSS: *Journal of the Folk-Song Society*.
ECS: Lucy E. Broadwood and J. A. Fuller Maitland (eds), *English County Songs* (London: Leadenhall Press; J. B. Cramer and Co.; Simpkin, Marshall, Hamilton, Kent, and Co., 1893).

'Among the Green Hay' (Roud 855)	SBG/1/2/770
'Banks of Sweet Dundee' (Roud 148)	LEB/2/68
'Banks of Sweet Primroses' (Roud 586)	LEB/2/66; *JFSS*, 4.2 (no. 15) (1910), 124
'Barbara Allen' (Roud 54, Child 84)	LEB/2/66; *JFSS*, 1.5 (1904), 266–67
'Fair Maid Walking in her Garden' (Roud 264)	*JFSS* 4.2 (no. 15) (1910), 127–29
'How Sweet in the Woodlands' (Roud 13775)	LEB/2/67
'I Courted a Bonny Lass; or, The False Lover' (Roud 154)	LEB/2/67; LEB/2/68
'In Rochester City' (Roud 1651)	LEB/2/68; *JFSS*, 1.4 (1902), 224–25
'Jenny of the Moor' (Roud 581)	LEB/2/66
'My Bonny Bonny Boy' (Roud 293)	LEB/2/66; *ECS*, pp. 146–47
'Nothing Else to Do' (Roud 1265)	LEB/2/68; SBG/1/2/433
'Oh Why Was I Born to Be Tormented So' (Roud 2463)	LEB/2/67
'Ploughing Song' (Roud 346)	LEB/2/66; *ECS*, p. 65
'The Garland of Love' (Roud 1247)	LEB/2/68
'The Oyster Girl' (Roud 875)	LEB/2/68
'When the Morn Stands on Tiptoe' (Roud 24896)	LEB/2/67

'Of Her He Asked No Leave'

DIANA COLES

It is a truism to say that folk songs reflect the social attitudes and concerns that prevailed at the time of their composition. Yesterday's burning issue may well become tomorrow's irrelevance. Broadsides, to some degree, were the tabloids of their day, churned out for mass consumption, often with little or no literary merit. Many of the songs that were written about a specific event have disappeared into total obscurity. Those garnered into published collections, most notably by Francis James Child, have become a go-to resource for singers looking for new material.

In the wake of what seems a never-ending stream of unpleasant revelations about the sexual abuses perpetrated by those in high places, and the recent 'MeToo' campaign, it is interesting to consider how the subject of sexual violence against women has been dealt with in the vernacular literature of the past and how this reflects (or otherwise) general social attitudes as manifested in the codified law, in the practice of the judicial system, and in literature and mythology. Furthermore, we may consider how changing attitudes towards women's rights have altered, and are continuing to alter, the way in which performers approach such songs.

Historically, and particularly after the Norman invasion, women have not been well served by either the legislature or those in charge of administering the law when it comes to sexual crimes against the person. Prior to the Norman Conquest, England was under Saxon and, in some areas, Viking legislation. Although the Vikings' reputation towards women is less than salubrious, their behaviour at home paints a different picture. Men and women had defined and very different social roles, but they were treated equally under the law. Harming a woman was regarded as dishonourable. Touching a woman without her consent was a civil offence which could in extreme cases lead to the offender being outlawed from society. Saxons, like Vikings, did not operate a prison system. Most offences were punished by fines, with the death penalty for the most serious crimes. Assault on a woman was subject to a legal penalty which was made up partly of compensation to the victim and partly of a much larger fine that went to the crown. In the case of a slave, the compensation was paid to her master. The amount of the fine and compensation varied according to the status of the woman. Thus in the ninth century the fine for rape of a free woman was 120*s*., with a compensation payment of 60*s*., while for a slave the amounts were 60*s*. and 5*s*., respectively. However if the woman was not a virgin the compensation was halved.[1]

The Normans' attitude towards women was largely derived from Roman law. Under the feudal system, as Sellar and Yeatman expressed it, 'everybody had to belong to somebody else, and everybody else to the king'.[2] An attack on a gentlewoman was regarded primarily as damaging male property. Inheritances were very much on the minds of the lawmakers who drew up the thirteenth-century Statutes of Westminster. Although forced marriages were not, strictly speaking, legal, in fact men considered it their right to marry off their daughters as they chose. The feelings of the assaulted woman were a lesser concern, although the law strongly condemned the deflowering of virgins since it seriously lowered their marketable value. The crime of rapine meant the carrying off by force of either a woman or inanimate property. The term *rapuit* in legal documents can mean either abduction or rape.[3] In 1380, Chaucer was released by Cecilia Champaigne from any legal actions relating to her ravishment. It is unclear whether this refers to a brutal attack or a romantic elopement. Of 1,194 cases concerning *rapuit* that came to the courts between the thirteenth and fifteenth centuries, 556 were cases of abduction, 108 were rapes, and in 527 cases it is impossible to be clear what was involved.

'Eppie Moray' (Child 223) is an account of a failed abduction. Eppie Moray is kidnapped by a gang of twenty-four armed men. They take her to the minister's house and demand that he marry her to Willie. When she makes her objection plain, the minister refuses. Willie then attempts to take her to bed. However, Eppie continues to resist him and in the morning he is forced to let her go home 'a maiden as I cam'. The song would appear to date from the post-medieval period – Maidment, who published the ballad in 1842, considered it to be at least a century old at that time – but the theme of abduction by force of an heiress could have come from a much earlier period. Women who consented to their abduction – who chose

---

[1] C. Hough and E. Kennedy, 'Alfred's *Domboc* and the Language of Rape: A Reconsideration of Alfred ch. 11', *Medium Aevum*, 66 (1997), 1–27.

[2] W. C. Sellar and R. J. Yeatman, *1066 and All That* (London: Methuen, 1930).

[3] Corinne J. Saunders, *Rape and Ravishment in the Literature of Medieval England* (Cambridge: D. S. Brewer, 2001), pp. 33–75.

to elope with the man of their choice against the wishes of their parent or guardian – were seen as equally culpable. Furthermore, following the teaching of Galen, there was a widespread belief that rape could never result in pregnancy – a folk myth, incidentally, that has survived to the twenty-first century. Republican congressman Todd Aiken expressed the view in 2012 that 'If it's a legitimate rape the female body has ways to shut that whole thing down.'[4] It is interesting that he received more criticism for the term 'legitimate' applied to rape than for his perpetuation of a piece of totally unscientific nonsense. In historical terms, this myth meant that if a woman became pregnant as the result of a sexual assault it was considered to be a proven consensual act. We may also note that Eppie is able, somewhat improbably, successfully to resist her attacker even although he is surrounded by armed men and she is alone and defenceless.

In theory, punishment for sexual assaults on high-born women were severe. Under the laws of the early Normans a convicted rapist could be sentenced to castration and blinding. After the Statutes of Westminster the usual penalty was hanging, although for a number of years this was commuted to two years' imprisonment, before the death penalty was reintroduced. If the woman was prepared to marry her assailant, then in some circumstances the legal penalty could apparently be remitted. It has been suggested that it is this practice that is referred to in 'The Knight and Shepherd's Daughter' (Child 110). In this ballad the eponymous heroine runs to the king for redress and is awarded the hand of her attacker in marriage. From his surly reaction to being forced to accept a lower-class bride, one wonders whether her social advancement would prove worth it. In the seventeenth-century broadside versions, on their marriage she reveals that she is of a higher social class than he is.

The Roman Catholic church, with its broad streak of misogyny, had much to do with medieval attitudes towards the sexual treatment of women. While on the one hand church leaders placed a highly inflated value on female sexual purity, on the other hand they regarded women as vile daughters of Eve whose flagrant sexuality and lust were the undoing of mankind. There was a widespread belief among male writers that women who were forced into sexual acts by men generally 'enjoyed it really'. Christine de Pisan refuted this: 'Yet it grieveth me of that, that many men say that women would be ravished

---

[4] Quoted in J. Elijon and M. Schwirtz, 'Senate Candidate Provokes Ire with "legitimate rape" Comment', *New York Times*, 19 August 2012.

and it displeaseth them not though they say they contrary with their mouths. But it were a great thing to make me believe that it were agreeable to them.'[5]

The medieval church's attitude may be summed up as the only good woman is a virgin, preferably a dead virgin. The cult of the Virgin Mary was widespread, as was the veneration of saints. A number of saints gained their sanctity through the determination with which they defended their virginity from would-be ravishers.[6] St Lucy pulled out her own eyes to deter her suitor. St Agnes and St Agatha were both dispatched to brothels and suffered torture but remained undefiled, while St Uncumber (or Wilgefortis) grew a beard. The conflation of virginity with female chastity has persisted into very recent times. St Maria Goretti, an eleven-year-old girl, was stabbed to death by a neighbour during a sexual assault. She died in 1902 and was canonized in 1950. She was lauded by Pope John Paul II because 'she chose death when there was no other way to defend her virgin purity'.[7] It does seem that in Catholic mythology a virgin cannot be raped against her will, although she may be called upon to die as the alternative to losing her purity.

Detailed accounts of dealings in the English courts exist from the latter half of the seventeenth century and from these it is possible to build up some idea of how crimes of sexual assault were viewed and treated. They make for very unpleasant reading. From 1674 to 1699, of thirty-three cases of rape tried at the Old Bailey, sixteen of the accused were completely acquitted, while a further five were found guilty of a lesser charge of assault, even though four of these assaults were on children below the age of ten, one of whom was infected with gonorrhoea by her assailant. The remaining accused were found guilty and sentenced to death. At least seventeen of the victims were under ten, which was the age of consent at the time. Sadly, in an age when venereal disease was rife and it was believed that intercourse with a virgin was a way to cure it, some of the girls were used for that purpose. In not one of the cases involving an adult was the accused convicted – reasons being variously that she did not complain until the next day, that the court believed it was a ploy to get money, that

---

[5] Christine de Pisan, *The Book of Ladies* (1405), trans. and ed. R. Brown-Grant (London: Penguin, 1999).

[6] K. A. Winstead, *Virgin Martyrs: Legends of Sainthood in Late Medieval England* (Ithaca, NY: Cornell University Press, 2018); E. Abbott, *A History of Celibacy* (Cambridge: Lutterworth Press, 2001).

[7] James Likoudis, 'Patroness of Purity – St Maria Goretti, Virgin and Martyr' https://www.mariagoretti.org/likoudisarticle4.htm.

the complainant had consented, or that she was a loose-living woman who could not be believed.

A broadside from the seventeenth century demonstrates the extent to which women were held to blame for what was at the time termed seduction but would generally today be considered rape. *The Windsor Frolick; or, A Hue and Cry after a Couple of Maiden-heads* relates how a pair of innocent country girls try to resist drinking alcohol.[8] Will, however, talks them into drinking far too much and when they are unconscious invites his friend to join in the fun. The girls are regarded as objects of ridicule rather than compassion:

> But they at length both consented,
> and with him they briskly go,
> For which at last they repented,
> and would it had not been so,
> But alas their wishes are vain,
> for what they cannot recall,
> And though they still sigh and complain
> they must be laught at by all.

The presumption that the girls were largely to blame has, sadly, changed very little in the minds of a proportion of the population. A 2006 poll revealed that around one third of people believed a woman was partially or totally responsible for being raped if she was drunk.[9]

The prosecution at the Old Bailey of Stephen Arrowsmith in 1678 for raping nine-year-old Elizabeth Hopkins illustrates the unwillingness of juries to convict. Arrowsmith was the apprentice of Elizabeth's father and the child said that he had been abusing her over a period of six months or so. One of the assaults had actually been witnessed by another child, and Elizabeth showed signs of physical damage and venereal disease. Arrowsmith pleaded not guilty and said that sex had been consensual. The judge pointed out that as she was under the age of consent this was irrelevant. The jury were sent out to consider their verdict and came back with 'not guilty', largely because one of their number, an apothecary, gave it as his professional opinion that 'a child of those years could not be ravished'. The judge asked why then had Parliament passed a law against it? and sent them off to think again. The judge had declined to call either of the girls for cross-

---

[8] *The Windsor Frolick; or, A Hue and Cry after a Couple of Maiden-heads* (printed for J. Gilbertson, at the Sun and Bible, on London Bridge) [ESTC R234112].
[9] https://www.amnesty.org.uk/press-releases/icm-poll-shocking-numbers-girls-and-young-womens-rightss-rightss-rightss-rightss.

examination, but the court was informed that during the jurors' deliberations the girls were present. That was, of course, illegal. The jury blamed it on an officer of the court, who found himself in very hot water; the girls were sworn in as witnesses and gave their evidence; Arrowsmith was found guilty and duly hanged at Tyburn. The trial was a remarkably swift affair by modern standards, being completed in less than a day.[10]

The difficulty of obtaining a conviction is not wholly unexpected. With no forensic evidence to go on, and with the myth still prevalent even today that women are wont to cry rape either for financial gain or out of spite, it is not surprising that juries were unwilling to send men to the gallows unless the victim's credentials were unassailable. The seventeenth-century jurist Sir Matthew Hale warned that jurors should 'be the more cautious upon trials of offenses of this nature [. . .] the heinousness of the offense many times transporting the judge and the jury with so much indignation, that they are over hastily carried to the conviction of the person accused thereof, by the confident testimony sometimes of false and malicious witnesses'.[11] Lord Hale, incidentally, was responsible for the legal position that rape within marriage was not possible, since 'by their mutual matrimonial consent and contract the wife hath given up herself in this kind unto her husband which she cannot retract'.[12]

Although the law stated that a prostitute had the same right to redress for sexual assault as a virgin, the character of the complainant continued to be a major factor in deciding whether a charge should be upheld. The situation changed but little when the death penalty for rape was abolished in 1841. Between 1842 and 1851 there were 130 trials for rape recorded at the Old Bailey. Of these, in sixty cases the defendants were were acquitted, while nine were found guilty of the lesser charge of assault. The authorities were only slightly more willing to press charges, and juries to convict, when prison or transportation replaced the rope. The victims whose cases came to court were still primarily children, who could not possibly be regarded as complicit.

And what of the Victorian era when sexual licence came to be so frowned upon? Along with their highly sentimentalized view of women and motherhood and the idealized view of the 'Angel in the

---

[10] Proceedings of the Old Bailey, t16781211e-2 https://www.oldbaileyonline.org/.

[11] Sir Matthew Hale, *The History of the Pleas of the Crown*, ed. Sollom Emlyn, George Wilson, and Thomas Dogherty, new edn, 2 vols (London, 1800), I, 636.

[12] Rebecca M. Ryan, 'The Sex Right: A Legal History of the Marital Rape Exemption', *Law & Social Inquiry*. (Blackwell Publishing, 1995).

House', Victorians could argue that working-class women were 'merely biological females who hardly deserve being called women at all'.[13] The Victorian ethos maintained that gentlemen did not treat women badly, ergo if a gentleman was accused of rape the accuser must be lying. On one occasion, Lord Chief Justice Alexander Cockburn refused to hear evidence about the rape of a young maidservant, despite her serious injuries, on the grounds that he did not believe that a respectably married man with a middle-class wife and children would lower himself to assaulting a menial. Justice Henry Manisley summarily dismissed every single case of rape on the assize calendar without any consideration of the evidence. Magistrates continued to dismiss most rape cases before they came before a jury, as they had done in the eighteenth century, even though this was beyond their legal capacity. Carolyn Conley has analysed the statistics from court records in Kent and concludes that only 21 per cent of men accused of rape stood trial, and some of those were on reduced charges. Even when they went to trial, the conviction rate was disproportionately low, at just 40 per cent, while for other felonies it stood at 85 per cent.[14]

Nevertheless, there are a number of broadsides from the period that deal with the problem of male sexual violence towards females. First, there are a broadsides written as reportage of actual crimes – *The Horrid Outrage and Murder of a Female, at Cleveland*, for example, which carried a prose account followed by the ballad. The rape and murder of Emily Holland, aged seven, in Blackburn in 1876 was reported in a series of broadsides which recounted the crime, the apprehension and trial of Fish, the perpetrator, and gave an account of his execution. Similarly, we have broadside accounts of *A Horrible Outrage and Murder at Little Staunton, Bedfordshire*; *The Life, Trial and Execution of Alex Richmond Who Suffered in Derby on Monday Last for a Rape and Murder Committed on the Body of Mary Long at Harley Green near Derby*; and *A Horrid Murder at Purfleet*, with a prose introduction and what purports to be 'an affecting copy of verses written by the unfortunate youth'. These sensational accounts are, like much of what appears in the tabloid press today, both badly written and inaccurate. They all dwell on the horrid murder and, in deference to Victorian sensibilities, the aspect of sexual assault is alluded to rather than made explicit.

---

[13] Carolyn A. Conley, 'Rape and Justice in Victorian England', *Victorian Studies*, 29 (1986) 519–36 (p. 530).

[14] Conley, 'Rape and Justice in Victorian England', p. 521.

One of the most extreme examples of biased and manipulative reporting concerns the *cause célèbre* of Mary Ashford who, in 1817, was found drowned in a pit after having spent the previous evening with a man at a dance. The ballad of *Mary Ashford's Tragedy* is written as though by her ghost.[15] She says that she had been molested by this man, who then drowned her when she threatened to bring him to justice, and calls for people to take action against her attacker:

Extirpate the wretch if the laws won[']t revenge,
And him from society spurn,
May remorse gnaw his soul,
And his time quickly roll,
T[e]ll him wihout reprieve,
Hell doth him receive,
And no humane breast for him mourn.

The wretch in question was one Abraham Thornton, who was arrested for her murder. He had been seen leaving the dance with Mary and admitted that they had had sex, but claimed it was consensual, and was acquitted of the rape and murder. The evidence for his innocence is convincing and Mary's death was almost certainly accidental. However, there was a campaign to overturn the verdict and Mary's brother was funded to bring an appeal of murder against Thornton, an antiquated legal process which was actually abolished as a result of this trial. Thornton responded by challenging Ashford to trial by conduct. Ashford declined and after a great deal of legal wrangling Thornton was freed. However, public feeling against him, whipped up by the press, remained so strong that he emigrated to the United States.

Besides the sensationalism of the rape and murder ballads, the issue of sexual violence against women was dealt with in other contemporary broadsides. George Brown, a London writer of the 1830s with twenty-two known ballads to his credit, and whose songs show him to be in sympathy with society's underdogs, wrote *The Cruel Sea-Captain and Nancy of Yarmouth*.[16] In this ballad, when the sea captain, armed with a pistol in each hand, orders Nancy to yield up

---

[15] *Mary Ashford's Tragedy, Who Was Ravished and Murdered at Erdington, near Birmingham, on the 27th Day of May 1817* (Jackson & Son, late J. Russell, printer, Moore Street, Birmingham; travellers supplied) [Oxford, Bodleian Library, Firth c.17(186)].

[16] James Hepburn, *A Book of Scattered Leaves: Poetry of Poverty in Broadside Ballads of Nineteenth-Century England*, 2 vols (Lewisburg: Bucknell University Press, 2000), pp. 46–49.

her virtue or drink the poison he has provided, she quickly shows herself to be no pushover:

> That instant pretty Nancy she turn'd with a frown,
> She seized both the pistols and knock'd Edward down.
> Lay there, cruel creature – pretty Nancy she said,
> You may take your strong poison, still Nancy's a maid.

The Model Workhouse Master! tells how the master uses his position to take advantage of the young women in the workhouse – no doubt a reflection of actual practice.[17] The arch tone of the ballad condemns the man, but falls short of any real sympathy for the young women:

> He went too far, – he was forced to strike it,
> The girls never scream'd because they liked it,
> He is a nice man for all the ladies,
> He'll soon fill the nursery with little babies.

Songs about Colonel Valentine Baker similarly trivialize the issue. Colonel (or Pasha) Baker, commander of the 10th Hussars, was a highly respected military man and a close friend of the Prince of Wales. In 1875, he was travelling by train from Portsmouth to London in a first-class carriage. The only other person in the carriage was a young lady, 21-year-old Rebecca Dickenson. The colonel assaulted her, kissing her while putting his hand inside her underwear. She avoided him by opening the door of the train and clinging to the running-board. A railway worker spotted her and the train was stopped; she was escorted to a place of safety, and Baker was subsequently arrested and charged with attempted rape. The ensuing scandal was massive. The trial judge summed up by saying that he could find no evidence of attempt to ravish and that the colonel had tried to 'win the girl's consent to intercourse by exciting her passions'. The colonel was found guilty of indecent assault, fined £500, and imprisoned for one year. This event resulted in popular songs to commemorate the affair. But although the young lady concerned was frightened enough by the attack to place herself in an extremely dangerous position, the songs largely treat the whole affair as a source of amusement. *The Lamentation of a Naughty Colonel* concludes:

> If courting's such a sin, I never will again,
> Make love, though I think it is a shame,

---

[17] *The Model Workhouse Master!* [Oxford, Bodleian Library, Harding B 13(111)].

As in prison I do sit, I never shall forget,
That kissing in the railway train.[18]

Likewise, *The Colonel and the Lady* has:

When a gent gets in a railway train,
Some time the ladies they will complain,
Some people say that it is a shame,
To try and kiss the lady,
Some girls we know love soldiers tall,
Their military walk, moustaches and all,
This case I cannot make out at all,
About the colonel and the lady,
Perhaps he only trod upon her dress,
If he did it[']s hard you must confess,
He has got himself into a pretty mess,
Through kissing this young lady.[19]

Nevertheless, had Rebecca not been a 'lady', the crime against her would have been treated even less seriously.

In a case paralleling that of Baker, a retired army captain was found guilty of raping a servant girl in a railway carriage. His sentence was a mere three months. Young women servants were particularly vulnerable to sexual assault. The law rarely supported them and on the occasions when a judgement went in their favour the sentences against their assailants were disproportionately light. *Anne Devine, the Morpeth Servant* tells how a servant girl left her post when her master moved her bed into his room. The magistrates, having found her employer not guilty of rape, generously decided not to send her to prison for leaving her post before her indentured time was up, but did order her to forfeit all her wages:

It[']s hard that a young girl she must leave her place
Because she'll not submit for to suffer disgrace,
And be robbed of her wages if she should refuse,
[I]t[']s time some fresh men were in other men[']s shoes.[20]

In Kent, a young servant girl left her employment after being repeatedly attacked by her employer. She was supported in bringing

---

[18] *The Lamentation of a Naughty Colonel* (Disley, printer, London) [Oxford, Bodleian Library, Harding B 11(2046), Harding B 20(260)].

[19] *The Colonel and the Lady* [Oxford, Bodleian Library, Johnson Ballads 2409].

[20] *Anne Devine, the Morpeth Servant* [Oxford, Bodleian Library, Harding B 13(140)].

charges against him by the Society for the Protection of Women and Children, a philanthropic organization devoted primarily to bringing in legislation to prevent the trafficking of women. Despite this support, the magistrates threw out the case and then fined the young woman because she had been absent from service without permission.

None of these songs enjoys wide circulation today. In the case of the abused and murdered children it is easy to understand why. Such atrocities are regarded with horror in modern society (despite the widespread occurrence of child abuse) and it would be regarded as in extremely bad taste to sing about them. It is less clear why songs like *Anne Devine, the Morpeth Servant* are not sung – they have as much relevance to modern life as the numerous poaching songs in singers' repertoires.

What then of the classical ballads, those in the Child collection? A number of them deal specifically or incidentally with sexual abuse and the exploitation of women. 'Prince Heathen' (Child 104), for example, has a narrative so unpleasant that personally I have long found it almost unbearable to listen to. A man is rejected by a woman and then punishes her by slaughtering her family and raping, impregnating, imprisoning, and starving her. She refuses to be broken, so he forces her to give birth in public, while subjecting her to derision and humiliation, and only relents when she complains that her newborn baby has nothing but a horse-blanket for wrapping. Child's comments on it are sketchy. I have heard it suggested that this was possibly an 'atrocity story', a warning about how 'heathens' (whatever non-Christian group might have been intended) behave – similar perhaps to 'Sir Hugh'. Martin Carthy, who performs a version that owes much to A. L. Lloyd, comments: 'It's always been a source of bewilderment to much of humanity as to why people behave in such a disgusting way to other people, and that's why there are songs like "*Prince Heathen*".'[21]

No performer renders that ballad as light-hearted. Other songs however, treat the subject of raping virgins with a merry twinkle in the eye. 'The Twa Magicians' (Child 44), another song that Lloyd adapted, relates the refusal of a smith with magical powers to take 'no' for an answer. The song strongly suggests that since her objection is based on social snobbery the lady deserves her fate. Many contemporary performers apparently find no problem with this. The controversy about this song that rages on internet forums includes the view that it is not about rape at all but rather 'a test performed by the lady to

---

[21] Martin Carthy, *Signs of Life*, CD (Topic TSCD503, 1998).

ensure that the smith is worthy of her', or alternatively that it is a metaphor for summer conquering winter. That view, which sees the song as having deep roots in prehistoric ritual, has no doubt gained weight from Lloyd's reference to 'the Bronze Age notion of the smith as an essentially superhuman being'.[22] The discomfort of modern audiences has been attributed to the song being performed on 'college campuses where political correctness (and the cult of feminine victimhood) loom large'.[23] The contemporary group Lady Maisery, however, have reworked the ending, using Child's notes on European variants on the story, saying they 'were uncomfortable with the British version [. . .] because of the predatory feel and connotations of sexual harassment'.[24] Kim Edgar and Joshua Purnell have also rewritten the words to allow the lady to emerge from the duel victorious.

The eponymous protagonist of 'Tam Lin' (Child 39) appears in some of the fourteen variants printed by Child to have assaulted Janet against her will. For instance, Child 39 D (from Motherwell's MS) reads:

> He took her by the milk-white hand,
> And by the grass green sleeve,
> And laid her low down on the flowers,
> At her he asked no leave.
>
> The lady blushed and sourly frowned,
> And she did think great shame [. . .]

In other versions this is omitted. Singers have shown the same ambivalence. The well-known recording by Fairport Convention excludes this stanza, while both Anne Briggs and Steeleye Span retain it. It does not seem in any event that any blame is allowed to attach to Tam Lin.

'Glasgerion' (Child 67), better known from A. L. Lloyd's adaptation as 'Jack Orion', is a king's son and master harper. In this ballad it is the foot-page who takes advantage of the princess by pretending to be his master. When it becomes apparent what has happened, so appalled is she at having lain with a 'churl' that she kills herself. Glasgerion goes home, hangs or beheads the boy, and falls on his own sword. Now, under the Sexual Offences Act (2004) the boy's action would constitute rape, because 'The defendant intentionally

---

22 A. L. Lloyd, *Folk Song in England* (London: Lawrence and Wishart, 1967), p. 154.

23 Robina, 'Twa Magicians' thread, @mudcat.org (2001).

24 Lady Maisery, *Mayday*, CD (RootBeat Records RBRCD19, 2013).

induced the complainant to consent to the relevant act by impersonating a person known personally to the complainant.' However, many performers seem to regard his behaviour as a mere peccadillo. Bert Lloyd wrote: 'Farm boys, tailors' apprentices, stable-grooms and other tricksters who overhear assignations and forestall the lover are standard stuff in folklore, but they don't usually come to such an unjustly sticky end as opportunistic Tom, the apprentice minstrel of our ballad.'[25]

Sadly, in the twenty-first century the situation remains murky. There is still little or no consensus even among women about what should constitute unacceptable attention, and men are complaining that assaults against them by women are being ignored or trivialized. Whenever allegations are made against a celebrity, a quick glance at social media reveals that the belief that accusations are largely made for personal gain is alive and flourishing, as is the notion that women are making a lot of fuss about nothing. Victim-blaming continues to thrive and although defence counsel are no longer allowed to ask routinely about a complainant's sexual history it does not always stop them doing so.

The police and the courts are taking complaints of sexual assault more seriously. In 2011/12, some 16,000 rapes and 22,100 sexual assaults were reported, of which 10.5 per cent were deemed non-crimes by the police. Of those that proceeded to court, 58 per cent were convicted, and all but forty received custodial sentences. However, in a survey it was found that on average one in twenty women between the ages of sixteen and fifty-nine had been the victim of an assault after the age of ten, and only 15 per cent of them had reported it to the police. The reasons they gave were embarrassment, feeling it was not worth reporting, feeling it was too personal, and thinking the police could not or would not take much action. Depressing as these figures are, we can be reasonably certain that in the past under-reporting would have been far higher, when a woman risked social opprobrium on the one hand and a legal system loaded against her on the other. And what of the songs and singers? The choices are to sing them anyway, to exclude them because of their offensiveness, or to tweak the words to bring them into line with contemporary sensibilities – the last being, I suspect, a process that has already been taking place in different ways over the years.

---

[25] A. L. Lloyd, *First Person: Some of his Favourite Folk Songs*, LP (Topic 12T118, 1966).

Tony Wales: Sussex Folk Song Collector in the 1950s and 1960s

SEAN GODDARD

The border areas of Kent, Sussex, and Surrey have long been a folk song collector's fertile hunting ground. In the mid-nineteenth century John Broadwood collected and published a small collection of songs,[1] and around the beginning of the twentieth Ralph Vaughan Williams, Lucy Broadwood, and Dorothy Marshall also collected and published songs from the area. These early collectors naturally used pen and paper to note the songs they found, but, as Bill Leader has commented, the advent of the tape recorder after the Second World War allowed almost anybody to record material.[2]

During the 1950s and 1960s collectors such as Mervyn Plunkett, Ken Stubbs, Reg Hall, Peter Kennedy, and Tony Wales all used tape recorders in this part of the country, but while material collected by the first four has been publicly available for some time,[3] the recordings made by Tony Wales have only recently been made generally accessible.[4] Sixty years on, the work of this post-war generation of collectors not only gives us hours of recordings which can be listened to with pleasure and profit, but it also forms the bedrock of much of our current knowledge of the subject. It is time we started looking at these collectors and their work more seriously. This paper introduces Tony Wales and explores how he became interested in folk music, how he went about his collecting work, and some of the singers and musicians he met.

---

[1] John Broadwood, *Old Sussex Songs, as Now Sung by the Peasantry of the Weald of Surrey and Sussex, and Collected by One Who Has Learnt Them by Hearing Them Sung Every Christmas* (London: Balls, [1843]).

[2] Pete Heywood, 'Bill Leader: 50 Years in the Recording Industry – Part 1', *The Living Tradition*, no. 68 (2006), 26–31 (p. 26).

[3] A range of material from this area is available on the *Voice of the People*, ed. Reg Hall, CDs (Topic TSCD651–670, 1998; TSCD671–672, 2012). Reg Hall's field recordings are available at the British Library https://sounds.bl.uk/World-and-traditional-music/Reg-Hall-Archive. Ken Stubbs's recordings are available at VWML. Some of Mervyn Plunkett's recordings are at the British Library.

[4] Sussex Traditions, A Window into the Traditional Culture of the County https://sussextraditions.org.

Anthony Wales was born on New Year's Eve 1924 and lived almost his entire life in Horsham. He married his wife Hilda in 1963, and died in 2002. The major development of his musical tastes took place in the 1950s, when he worked for a time at Andrew's record store. Like many of his generation, he became particularly fond of traditional jazz, followed by the blues, with leading performers such as Big Bill Broonzy and Josh White, and then discovered folk music.[5] He became involved with the Horsham branch of the International Friendship League (IFL) and this gave him contact with people from overseas and differing cultures. The League organized social gatherings and occasionally guests would perform their country's own music and songs. Realizing the importance of the music, in 1956 Tony purchased a portable clockwork tape recorder, a Butoba Export, to start recording it.[6]

Reading local history books, especially those by Henry Burstow,[7] and William Albery,[8] Tony became interested in local history, especially if it took a folkloric slant. Listening to BBC wireless programmes such as *As I Roved Out*,[9] which broadcast local songs and stories, Tony realized that people a generation or two older than himself offered the best opportunities for further research, and he considered that Horsham and the surrounding area might offer similar recording opportunities.

Tony started his recordings close to home. His mother Minnie knew some songs, as did Charlie and Marjorie Potter, who were fellow members of Horsham's Folk Dance Club.[10] He recorded all three in June 1956 and subsequently ventured further afield, recording Lewes singer George Townshend in 1957, and George Attrill at Fittleworth in 1958. In 1959, he went over the border to Godalming in Surrey and recorded Tinker Smith, and in 1960 he recorded Louie Fuller (Saunders) in Lingfield.[11]

Tony was aware that singers like his mother and the Potters had learned songs from their families, and there were others who, as part of the folk revival, had learned songs from books and media such as

---

[5] Tony Wales, interview with Sean Goddard, Horsham, 8 September 1996.

[6] Goddard interview.

[7] *Reminiscences of Horsham, being Recollections of Henry Burstow, the Celebrated Bellringer & Songsinger* (Horsham: Free Christian Church Book Society, 1911).

[8] William Albery, *A Parliamentary History of the Ancient Borough of Horsham, 1295–1885* (London: Longmans Green, 1927).

[9] Broadcast on the BBC Light Programme 1953–58 and presented by Peter Kennedy.

[10] Goddard interview.

[11] Details of recording dates and locations taken from the tape boxes.

radio and records. Some, like Tony and the Potters' son Terry, had learned in both ways. In 1958, he started the Horsham Songswappers, the first organized folk song club in Sussex, in the hope that he could bring them all together.[12] It was a success and in the next few years regular attendees included traditional singers and musicians Bob Blake, George Belton, and William Agate, along with revival singers Dave Toye, Clive Bennett, and Harry Mousdell.

Tony and his new colleagues organized three Horsham Folk Festivals. In 1961 and 1962 they were held at the Boys' Club in Hurst Road, and in 1963 at the Albion Hall in Albion Road.[13] All three festivals included both revivalist and traditional singers. Tony recorded some of the singers and to ensure the quality of the recordings he invested in a new tape recorder, a Ferrograph Series 4, a type used by the BBC. He made recordings of Cyril Phillips, Bob Blake, Scan Tester, and George Townshend, which subsequently appeared on the *Songs and Music of the Sussex Weald* reel-to-reel tape issued by the EFDSS in 1966.[14]

Many of the singers lived within easy reach of Horsham or appeared at the Horsham festivals, but Tony also went further afield. On one collecting trip in April 1959, when he visited Tinker Smith at Godalming, in Surrey, he was accompanied by Ken Stubbs,[15] and on another occasion he recorded William (Bill) Agate at Rusper. On at least one visit he was accompanied by Terry Potter, who recalls:

> Tony Wales and myself cycled over to record Bill Agate at his house in Rusper, approx. 5 to 6 miles from Horsham one early summer evening, with a green battery tape recorder strapped on the back of Tony's bike.
>
> Bill lived in a secluded spot deep in a forested area near Rusper village, and I remember him playing the tune 'Wearing of the Green' on his mouth organ, accompanying himself on tambourine, both instruments being held in one hand, while striking the tambourine with the other hand. He may have played other melodies on melodeon, and his wife may have been there also – but I can't remember for sure. I may also have joined in on my mouth organ and

---

[12] Clive Bennett, *Sussex Folk: The Folk Song Revival in Sussex* (Bakewell: Country Books, 2002), pp. 9–11.

[13] Bennett, *Sussex Folk*, pp. 10–11.

[14] Tony Wales, *Songs and Music of the Sussex Weald*, reel-to-reel tape (EFDSS Folktape FTA 102, 1966).

[15] https://sussextraditions.org/collection/?search_query=tinker%20smith.

perhaps Tony sang too. Later, circa 1962, Bill Agate played 'Wearing of the Green' at Horsham Folk Festival.[16]

Another significant singer he recorded was Ethel Powell, who lived in Portslade and later emigrated to Canada. She gave Tony over twenty songs, many learned as a child from her grandparents and extended family.[17] One song she sang, 'Battle of the Nile', appears to be the only recorded version of the song. Many of the singers Tony recorded were also recorded by other collectors, including Bob Copper, Ken Stubbs, Peter Kennedy, Reg Hall, Mervyn Plunkett, Brian Matthews, and Mike Yates.

In 1956, Tony, along with local guitarist Peter Baxter, recorded the master tape for the LP *Sussex Folk Songs and Ballads*, issued in 1957 by New York-based Folkways Records.[18] The record contained nineteen songs, nine of which he had recently collected, and the remainder either learned in childhood or from other sources:

- Five songs from 1956 recordings of Charlie and Marjorie Potter: 'Seventeen Come Sunday', 'Sing Ivy', 'Banks of the Sweet Dundee', 'Bailiff's Daughter of Islington', 'Henry Martin'.
- Three songs from his mother, Minnie Wales: 'Our Goodman', 'Piri-iri-igdum', 'Bryan O'Lynn'.
- One song from a 78 rpm record sung by the Burwash singer Albert Richardson: 'Sarie'.[19]
- One song from Percy Laker of Brighton: 'Buttercup Joe'.
- Three songs Tony had learned as a boy: 'To Be a Farmer's Boy', [selection of] 'Four Children's Singing Games', 'Richard of Taunton Deane'.
- Six songs from publications: 'On Christmas Night', 'I've Been to France', 'Horsham Boys', 'The Woodcutter', 'The Ploughboy', 'The Green Mossy Banks of the Lea'.

In 1961, Tony took on the role of Folk Shop Sales Manager at the English Folk Dance and Song Society (EFDSS), where he later became Press and Publications Officer. During his time there he was

---

[16] Personal communication (email), 18 September 2008.

[17] Ethel M. Powell, 'A Sussex Singing Family', *Folk Bag*, no. 4 (1961) https://sussextraditions.org/sustrad/media/Sussex_Singing_Family.pdf.

[18] Tony Wales, *Sussex Folk Songs and Ballads*, LP (Folkways FG 3315, 1957).

[19] 'Farmer's Boy' and 'Sarey' were recorded by Richardson and issued on Zonophone T6060, recorded December 1931. See also George Frampton, '. . . and they calls I Buttercup Joe': Albert Richardson, the Singing Sexton of Burwash, 1905–76. *Folk Music Journal*, 9.2 (2007), pp. 149–69.

responsible for the production of many EFDSS publications. In the early 1970s, under Tony's guidance, the EFDSS developed joint ventures with commercial publishers such as Galliard (an imprint of Stainer and Bell) and Chappell. The arrangement was that the EFDSS would supply content while the publishers covered the production and distribution costs – the profits would be shared.[20]

Under this scheme Tony was able in 1976 to publish his first book, *We Wunt be Druv*, a mixture of songs and folklore of Sussex.[21] A thousand copies were printed. Of the twelve songs in the book, eleven had been recorded by Tony between 1956 and 1964. This venture was slightly different from other EFDSS publications in that the profits were shared equally with Tony.[22] From 1963 until 1978, Tony edited the EFDSS's magazine, *English Dance & Song*, and was able to publish a number of Sussex songs and biographical articles about singers.[23]

Tony would use these songs and other folkloric material he had recorded in his numerous Sussex publications. Between 1976 and 2000, he published more than twenty works and edited many others, although they lacked rigorous scholarship since he always wrote for a popular audience. He also published some limited circulation items such as the *Folk Bag* and *Field and Furrow*, originally produced on a Gestetner cyclograph-type machine, and later on a photocopier, which were circulated among his friends. These would often include short articles containing Sussex songs and folklore.

The recordings

There was a long-standing connection between Tony and my father, John Goddard. Although they lived twenty-five miles apart, they had become friends during the 1950s, sharing an interest in folklore, song, and dance. Tony ran a folk dance band, the Derrydowners, which played in village halls in Sussex, and my father sometimes called barn dances with them. In the 1980s, while visiting the Vaughan Williams Memorial Library, I listened to some of Tony's recordings. When I told my father, he encouraged me to contact Tony and find out more. At that time Tony ran a second-hand book business called Field and Furrow which specialized in folklore and related subjects, and over the

20 Goddard interview.
21 Tony Wales, *We Wunt be Druv: Songs and Stories from Sussex* (London: Galliard and English Folk Dance and Song Society, 1976).
22 Goddard interview.
23 For example, Tony Wales, '"Buttercup Joe", Collected from P. Laker', *English Dance & Song*, 32.2 (1971), 61; Tony Wales, 'George Townsend of Sussex', *English Dance & Song*, 29.3 (1967), 70–73.

years I bought some books from him, which kept us in contact. So it was that in 1991 I purchased Tony's collection of eighty reel-to-reel tapes plus the Ferrograph tape recorder and microphone. The gentleman's agreement was that in due course the recordings would be made available to others. Sadly, this has taken more than twenty-five years, but a significant sample of Tony's location recordings, including songs, tunes, and other folkloric items, is now available on the Sussex Traditions website. It is likely that following the issue of the *Songs and Music of the Sussex Weald* in 1966 the tapes had remained largely unused until my purchase in 1991. I offered the recordings for use on Topic's *Voice of the People* project in the late 1990s, but better recordings of the singers and songs from other collectors such as Mervyn Plunkett were available. Otherwise, the tapes have remained in storage until now.

Like many of his generation of collectors, Tony was an amateur recorder working essentially on his own and financing his own activities. The recordings were all made within easy travelling distance of Horsham and Tony usually travelled by bus or bicycle. As Bill Leader explains, location recordings are made not in studios but in peoples' homes or other venues where the performers will feel more relaxed.[24] Tony was not particularly technologically minded and sometimes this resulted in poor microphone placement, making some of the recordings less than ideal. It was quite easy just to plug the microphone into the tape recorder, place it near the singer, and press record.[25] At times Tony was slow off the mark in pressing the record button and either missed the first few words or else there is a judder at the beginning.

At other times, the recording speed is 9.5 cm/s (3¾ inch/s), rather than 19 cm/s (7½ inch/s), and in consequence the frequency response suffers, as it is generally accepted that the faster the tape speed the better the quality of reproduction. The common domestic speed was 9.5 cm/s, whereas 19 cm/s was generally regarded as the slowest acceptable professional speed, and 38 cm/s (15 inch/s) was used for professional music recording and radio programmes.

The recordings were originally intended as an *aide-mémoire* for research for later writings and were not necessarily considered as being for broadcast or wider distribution, or even for permanent retention. That changed when recordings of traditional singers and other material that Tony had recorded at the Horsham Folk Festivals

---

[24] Pete Heywood, 'Bill Leader: 50 Years in the Recording Industry – Part 2', *The Living Tradition*, 70 (2006), 60–62 (p. 62).
[25] Heywood, 'Bill Leader – Part 1', p. 28.

were used on the *Songs and Music of the Sussex Weald* tape.[26] Throughout his life Tony continued to record people's memories and other events and sounds that interested him. Examples include Latin masses, the annual veteran car run from London to Brighton, his own singing experiments, often with Terry Potter, fairground organs, and radio programmes.

All his early recordings were made on reel-to-reel tape recorders, although he later switched to more user-friendly, but less high-quality, cassette tapes. The following paragraphs describe the machines and materials that were available to collectors like Tony. As first-hand knowledge of this technology passes from memory, it is important that the practical and technical details are recorded for the benefit of future researchers. The constraints of self-funding and lack of training, and the limitations of an emerging technology, all played a significant part in what was recorded and what was saved. The simple fact that tape was expensive for young enthusiasts meant that tapes were often carefully rationed and many were reused. Recording at a slow speed resulted in poorer quality but doubled the number of songs that could be captured on a limited budget.

Tony bought his first tape recorder in 1956, a stylish, up-to-date, German-made Butoba Export portable two-track mono machine.[27] Butoba was a manufacturer based in the Black Forest with a background in clockwork motors and was one of the first companies to develop a tape recorder for amateur use. Priced at DM750, it would have cost about £65 new, without microphone or tape. It was cheap in comparison with contemporary professional machines such as the Maihak Reportofon MMK 3, priced at approximately DM4000 (£342), or the Nagra II-CI. The price was kept low by including only the bare necessities, however; the early machines did not even have fast-forward or rewind functions. The Butoba was quite heavy, weighing in at 9.5 kg (21 lb), plus batteries, microphone, and tape. By way of comparison, the EMI Midget used by the BBC weighed only 6.6 kg (14 lb), but was more expensive. The Butoba was also heavier than the portable Uher 4000 series which was introduced in 1961 and weighed just 3 kg (6.6 lb). All the recordings made by Tony between 1956 and *c*.1960 were made on the Butoba.

---

26 Goddard interview.
27 I would like to thank Ricard Wanderlöf for background detail on Butoba tape recorders. Ricard has a website dedicated to these machines at http://butoba.net/homepage/r2rmain.html. See also https://www.radiomuseum.org/r/burger_export.html.

The Butoba had a clockwork motor which could run for about fifteen minutes at 19 cm/s, or about thirty minutes at 9.5 cm/s, and then needed to be rewound. It could record at either 19 cm/s or 9.5 cm/s. Due to the internal set-up, 19 cm/s was the more stable speed. The clockwork motor used a centrifugal governor and kept a stable speed until the tension in the springs dropped below the level required to maintain the correct speed, after which the speed would start to drop. It was, however, possible to wind the clockwork mechanism during recording in order to give additional recording time.

The frequency range of the Butoba recording at 19 cm/s peaked at around 13,000 kHz, but reduced to 5,000 kHz at 9.5 cm/s. Butoba did not make their own microphones but recommended suitable microphones from other companies, such as the small and light MD7 made by Laboratorium Wennebostel (a predecessor of Sennheiser), which is listed as an accessory in the manual. This microphone is described as a type designed for speech and dictation, with an advertised frequency response of 300 Hz to 6,000 kHz, although it might achieve frequencies beyond that range. The list price for a MD7 in 1953 was DM39 (£3 10s.).[28] This was the microphone that Tony used for his recordings.[29] It is likely that the characteristics of the available microphones limited the recording frequency and resulting sound to a greater extent than the tape recorder itself, especially if recording at 19 cm/s.

The maximum spool size used on the Butoba was 13 cm (5 inch) diameter. The spool size does not on its own define the recording time at a given speed – that is dependent on the length of the tape (*Table 1*). Tapes were available in different thicknesses with different playing times. Standard Play was the thickest, followed by Double Play, and Long Play. The thinner the tape, however, the more prone it was to jamming or breaking. As the Butoba was a two-track machine, recording on both sides of a 183 metre tape would give a total of thirty-two minutes of recording time. Although Tony used a variety of tape he generally used the widely available 'Scotch Boy' tape. *Table 1* shows the recording times for different lengths of tape. Although advertised as portable, the Butoba Export still required batteries or an external power supply. It required a 1.5 volt battery to power the valve heaters and a 100 volt supply for the amplifier circuitry. Batteries such

---

[28] https://www.radiomuseum.org/r/sennheiser_md7_md_7.html.
[29] Goddard interview.

as these would have been readily available as they were used for portable radios, but they were quite heavy.

Spool diameter	Tape length	Recording time per track at 9.5 cm/s	Recording time per reel at 9.5 cm/s	Recording time per track at 19 cm/s	Recording time per reel at 19 cm/s
13 cm	183 m (600 ft)	32 min	1 h 4 min	16 min	32 min
13 cm	275 m (900 ft)	48 min	1 h 36 min	24 min	48 min
17.75 cm	365 m (1,200 ft)	1 h 4 min	2 h 8 min	32 min	1 hr 4 min
17.75 cm	548 m (1,800 ft)	1 h 36 min	3 h 12 min	48 min	1 hr 36 min

Table 1. Tape lengths and recording times (approximate).

When Tony bought a Ferrograph Series 4 in 1961, it represented a major step forward.[30] It was a British-made tape recorder, used extensively by recording studios, the BBC, and similar organizations. It is not clear why he chose this particular model. He may have been influenced by the positive reports in *Which?* magazine, which reported in January of that year that it was one of only two machines that had a 'level meter' as opposed to a 'magic-eye', although it was also the most expensive tape recorder by £16.[31] In September *Which?* recorded it as the best buy in a subjective listening test,[32] although that report was published after he had bought the machine, which he had used at the Horsham Folk Festival in July. The Ferrograph weighed 23 kg (50 lb). The advantage of the Ferrograph over the Butoba Export was that it used larger 17.75 cm (7 inch) diameter tape spools.[33] Using 548 m (1,800 feet) of tape, that would permit forty-eight minutes of recording time per track at 19 cm/s, or 1 hour 36 minutes per spool if both tracks were used. Longer recording times could be obtained if

---

[30] Goddard, interview.

[31] 'Tape Recorders', *Which?*, January 1961, pp. 3–14 (p. 13); *The Guide to British Tape Recorders*, 5th edn (Rye: Jones, 2016), p. 307.

[32] 'Tape Recorders', *Which?*, September 1961, pp. 231–34 (pp. 233–34).

[33] *The Manual of the Ferrograph* (London: Ferrograph Recorder, 1961), p. 2.

thinner tape was used.[34] The Ferrograph used a regular mains power supply, and it was an 'all-in-one' unit with a small storage compartment for the mains lead and microphone, and so robust you could sit on it when it was not in use. Tony used a Grampian DP4 omnidirectional microphone, which, although not a top-quality microphone, was satisfactory, with an advertised frequency range wider than that of the previously used MD7 (*Table 2*).[35]

Frequency response	low (Hz)	high (kHz)
Butoba 9.5 cm/s	100	5,000
Butoba 19 cm/s	100	13,000
Ferrograph 9.5 cm/s	50	5,000
Ferrograph 19 cm/s	50	10,000
Laboratorium Wennebostel MD7 microphone	300	6,000
Grampian DP4L microphone	50	15,000

Table 2. Advertised frequency responses.

Tape recording in the 1950s and 1960s was an expensive hobby (*Table 3*). The average recorded salary of a Clerical Officer in the Civil Service in 1960 was £789 per annum (approximately £15 per week).[36] We do not know what was Tony's annual salary at this time, but it is likely that he was still living at home with his parents. The initial cost of the Butoba Export and the MD7 microphone would have been approximately £70. The cost of the Ferrograph Series 4 at £85,[37] plus the Grampian microphone at £7 11s.,[38] would have come to more than £90. In addition, there would have been purchase tax and the ongoing cost of tape.

Tony's contemporary Reg Hall confirms the relative costs.[39] Reg brought his first tape recorder in 1956, a Grundig which recorded at 9.5 cm/s, costing £54, which he bought on weekly payments (hire

---

[34] *Manual of the Ferrograph*, p. 2, indicates that the machine could take spools of a maximum 21 cm (8¼ inch) diameter, but Tony's collection does not contain any of that size.

[35] Grampian Reproducers, Technical Data Sheet (London: Grampian, [c.1960]).

[36] HC Deb, 29 November 2013 vol. 631, c42–43W.

[37] 'The Ferrograph Tradition', *Tape Recording and Hi Fi Magazine*, 4.1 (1960), 10; also *Which?*, September 1961, p. 233.

[38] H. Burrell Hadden, 'Equipment under Test: The Grampian DP4 Microphone', *Tape Recording and Hi Fi Magazine*, 4.1 (1960), 33.

[39] Reg Hall, interview with Sean Goddard, Denmark Hill, 1 January 2019.

purchase) of £1 per week. His weekly salary then was £7 10s., with outgoings of £1 for income tax and other deductions, £1 to his mother for board and lodging, £1 for bus fares, and £1 for cups of tea and food at work. This left £3 10s., of which £1 was spent on clothes and entertainment, while £1 went on payments for the tape recorder. A reel of 542 metre tape cost about £2.

Equipment	List price
Butoba Export	£65
Ferrograph Series 4	£85
MD7 microphone	£3 10s.
Grampian DP4L microphone, connector, and lead	£7 11s.
548 metres of tape	£2 10s.

Table 3. List prices of tape recorders, microphones, and tape (excluding purchase tax).

In 1957, 548 metres (1,800 ft) of Scotch Boy Extra Play (polyester base) tape cost £2 10s., while 365 metres (1,200 ft) of Scotch Boy 111A Standard (acetate base) cost £1 7s.[40] Extra Play tape was thinner than Standard tape. Tony used both.

As Tony was using a two-track machine, one minute of tape recording using Scotch Boy Standard tape would cost approximately 3d., while thirty-two minutes (one track) would cost 13s. 6d. (*Table 4*).

Type of tape	Cost of tape	Cost per min at 19 cm/s	Cost per 32 min at 19 cm/s
Scotch Boy Standard Play 365 m (1,200 ft)	£1 7s.	3d.	13s. 6d.
Scotch Boy Extra Play 548 m (1,800 ft)	£2 10s.	3.3d.	16s.

Table 4. Approximate costs of tape for recording.

Although Extra Play tape was more expensive, it had the advantage of recording for a longer period of time before needing to change the tape spool or track.

---

[40] 'Only 27/-? I'll take two', *Electrical and Radio Trading*, 9 November 1957, p. 42 (the original advert listed this as 1,800 feet).

When it comes to digitization, it is not all plain sailing. The type of machine used to play the tape may increase or reduce certain frequencies across the whole spectrum. The digitization process itself can also introduce new characteristics into, or remove unwanted ones from, the recording. One particular problem that is regularly encountered is tape machine speed. In the case of Tony's tapes, a different playback machine (Sony TC-766-2) was used by Jim Ward for the process. Assuming that the Sony was correctly calibrated to run at the correct speeds, and the Batoba and Ferrograph were likewise calibrated, then everything would be correct.

However, it only requires one machine to be running slightly fast or slow to introduce an error of pitch. One way to avoid this problem would have been to include the sound of a tuning fork or similar on the original recording, which would have made precise matching possible, but Tony, like others of his generation, could not have predicted what the future held. Alternatively, if the singers always sang in modern pitch, where A equals 440 Hz, then a correction could be applied – but I doubt if they did. As Jim Ward explains, a light touch of hum and hiss reduction, equalization, speed correction (where evidently necessary), and adjustment of volume levels has been applied to the recordings now available on the Sussex Traditions website in order to ensure that recordings that are now fifty years old are in an acceptable state for modern listeners.[41]

We are fortunate that enthusiastic collectors like Tony were able to self-fund their activities in the 1950s and 1960s, in small geographical areas. They have left us with an interesting, if sometimes incomplete, record of what took place at that time. Much has been written about the songs and the people who sang them, but little research has been published regarding the recording equipment the collectors used, which remains an area for further research.[42]

---

[41] Personal communication (email), 8 September 2018.
[42] I would like to thank Ricard Wanderlöf who helped with my Butoba tape recorder enquiries, and Barry Jones who answered my enquiries regarding the Ferrograph and recording tapes.

Postscript

At the Folk Song Conference, the author played the following musical examples:

- Charlie and Marjorie Potter singing 'Seventeen Come Sunday' – possibly the first song that Tony recorded on the Butoba, on 26 June 1956.[43]
- George Attrill singing 'The Nutting Girl' – a recording made at George's home in Fittleworth on 20 July 1958 using the Butoba.[44]
- Cyril Phillip singing 'Oi Come from the Country Me Name It Is Giles' – recording made using the Ferrograph at the Horsham Folk Festival on 29 July 1961.[45]
- William Agate playing 'Cock of the North' on the mouth organ and tambourine – recorded at William's house, Rusper, on 10 July 1959 using the Butoba. If you listen carefully to this recording, you can hear Tony humming along. [46]

---

[43] https://sussextraditions.org/record/seventeen-come-sunday-8/.

[44] https://sussextraditions.org/record/nutting-girl-the/.

[45] https://sussextraditions.org/record/farmer-giles-4/.

[46] https://sussextraditions.org/record/cock-of-the-north-2/.

Songs for the Death of an Angel: Traditional Music in Mesoamerica

GABRIELA HENRÍQUEZ

An angel gone too soon

The main focus of this article is a musical and social study of the traditional songs known as *parabienes* or *cantos de angelito* (little angel's songs), which are performed on the occasion of the death of an infant. These folk tunes have two main purposes. The first is to help the family and the community during the grieving process, since the idea of the purity of a child's soul remains present throughout the entire wake. The key to understanding this tradition is the Catholic belief in the soul, or human spirit, as something that is not material but has the capacity of thinking and acting by itself once it has surrendered its human condition. The second purpose of these tunes is strongly linked to the idea of the soul of an infant as something ethereal and pure which has no sin in it but which has to be reminded to go back to its place of origin – to its heavenly condition, to the presence of God – where it will become an angel, whose duty will be to preserve its family from any harm and to intercede for them before the almighty Creator.

This type of song can be found across a wide geographic territory which stretches from the southern United States to South America, and connects with a similar musical tradition in the Caribbean islands and Spain. In this paper I have mainly focused on the tradition still alive in the Mesoamerican area, which includes the countries of Mexico, Guatemala, El Salvador, and Honduras, a region that exhibits great cultural homogeneity.

At the beginning of this investigation the following questions emerged. Up to what age is one a child? What is the conception of a child according to the culture we are studying? What happens when a child dies in an orphanage or foster home? How do the concepts of social and economic class influence the festivity? Why is the popular religiosity of a human group so important in the process of enculturation of children attending the wake?

To answer these questions we proposed two main objectives. The first was to get to know what these types of tunes consist of, analysing them from an ethnomusicological and anthropological perspective, and understanding their social role and the religious views of their performers. The second main purpose was to understand how music acts as a therapeutic element during the grieving process. Four specific tasks were undertaken: a historical search into the possible origins of these songs; musical and textual comparisons of the songs found in the different regions mentioned above; musical transcriptions of the songs; and finally, it was considered important to try to understand the joyful meaning of these traditional songs.

The information used in this research was collected from fieldwork conducted mainly in the central and western areas of El Salvador. This included twelve different interviews with performers – people who have heard these songs at some point in their lives, and people who have described how these songs have helped them in the process of grieving for the death of a child. In addition to the data obtained during these meetings, more information has been collected thanks to the support of scholars from Mexico, El Salvador, Peru, Colombia, and Spain. Our analysis is based on documentary records, including baptism and death certificates, and on the study of written sources such as songbooks.[1]

Previous studies of this cultural and musical phenomenon have been concentrated in Mexico, Argentina, and Peru, while in the area of Mesoamerica research has been carried out from a purely anthropological perspective, leaving aside the question of the music.[2] The passage of time and the possible disappearance of these songs have been the main motivations for carrying out this study.

This angel belongs to heaven

Since pre-colonial times it has been common in Latin America to find expressions of fascination with the phenomenon of death. The death of a child, in many cases, is conceived as a merry occasion according to the Christian beliefs of the community. People tend to believe that the soul of a child is pure and therefore goes directly to God and becomes an angel that will watch over their family. One of the most important elements within these celebrations is the music, specifically the songs called *cantos de angelitos*, which are used to console the

---

[1] Francisco Espinosa, *Folklore musical salvadoreño: Melodías regionales* (El Salvador: Departamento de música Rodolfo A. Goldschmidt, 1949), p. 8.

[2] Juan Antonio Flores Martos and Luisa Abad Gonzáles, *Etnografía de la muerte y las culturas en América Latina* (Cuenca: Ediciones de la Universidad de Castilla y La Mancha, 2007); Jaume Bartulá Janot and Andrés Payà Rico, 'La cultura lúdica en los rituales funerarios de Iberoamérica: Los juegos de velorio', *Studium: Revista de humanidades*, 20 (2014), 167–88.

grieving family and, at the same time, serve as a form of farewell expression.

Even though these celebrations of death are now perceived from a Catholic perspective, we found some clues as to how the indigenous communities of the sixteenth century celebrated death. Diego García de Palacio, the sixteenth-century Spanish naval engineer, explorer, and researcher in the Viceroyalty of New Spain, wrote in his letters about the Mesoamerican cultures:

> They made two solemn sacrifices every year, by day; the one at the beginning of winter, and the other at the beginning of summer; and this sacrifice was hidden, that only *caciques* and important members of the community saw it, and it was inside the house where they prayed, and those who sacrificed for this sacrifice were boys from six years old to twelve.[3]

From this statement we can conclude that children were indeed considered as something precious, something worth gifting to the deities.

A second clue can be found in a book called *Historia de las Indias de Nueva España e Islas de Tierra Firme* by Diego Duran, Dominican friar and author of one of the earliest Western books on the history and culture of the Aztecs. There he describes a ceremony in which a boy and a girl were killed in honour of two hills, Tlaloc and Matlalcueye, the children being offered along with food and blood from their bodies. In the same chronicle Durán writes about how the Mesoamerican cultures had a festival called *Miccailhuitontli*, which can be translated from the Nahuatl into English as 'party for the little deceased, that was celebrated with great joy'. However, even though we have found these descriptions of how Mesoamerican cultures used to live, we could not find a written source that mentioned the performance of songs during these festivities.

The genesis of these celebrations is not entirely clear. We can suggest three hypotheses about their possible origins. The first is that these rituals and songs were introduced into America by African slaves. This hypothesis is supported by the fact that similar songs have been found in some areas that were heavily influenced by African cultures, such as the Caribbean islands and Colombia. The two further hypotheses are linked. One is that these rituals were pre-colonial

---

[3] Diego García de Palacio, *Cartas de relación del oidor Diego García de Palacio* (El Salvador: Dirección de publicaciones e impresos, 1525), p. 48.

celebrations that indigenous slaves brought with them to Spain; the other is that the words of these songs were adaptations of the Psalms made by religious orders in Spain, intended for the indoctrination of those new arrivals.

Songs for the death of an angel

The wake comprises a great number of symbols, which vary according to the economic capacity of the family of the deceased child, but which are fairly homogeneous throughout Latin America and Spain.[4] Among the most important symbols are the white clothes in which the child is dressed, the white coffin in which it is laid down, the festive dances and songs accompanied by stringed instruments, and the active participation of children in the celebration.

In the case of El Salvador, which is a fairly homogeneous society within a limited territory, we find that there is not a great difference in the way the songs are performed. The melody remains identical throughout the whole territory, maintaining an accompaniment of guitars and double basses. Through fieldwork we have been able to identify three different types of text, although the D-major element, tempo, ternary rhythm, and harmonic progression of dominant and tonic remain as shared characteristics.

(1) The first text was collected in Cojutepeque, in the department of Cuscatlán, in the central region of El Salvador. This text recounts the action from an external perspective, because it tells us what the singer is observing:

Si he venido a esta casa	If I've come to this house
Sin que me hayan convidado	Without being invited
A cantar los parabienes	To sing the compliments
A este niño amortajado.	To this shrouded child.
No llores madre amorosa	Do not cry loving mother
No llores con desconsuelo	Do not cry with grief
Que por el amor que tienes	That for the love that you have
No puedo dentrar al cielo.	I cannot go to heaven.
A las cuatro de la mañana	At four in the morning
Este niño falleció	This child died
La madrina y el padrino	The godmother and the godfather
La guirnalda le regaló.	The garland gave him.

---

[4] Gutierre Aceves, *El arte ritual de la muerte niña* (México: Artes de México, 1992).

Que dichoso es este niño	How happy is this child
Que nació para ir al cielo	Who was born to go to heaven
Más dichosa es la hora	Blessed is the hour
En que el Señor se lo llevó.	In which the Lord took him.
Ya con esta me despido	With this I say goodbye
Con ramitos de aceituno	With an olive branch
Y aquí me voy despidiendo	And here I am saying goodbye
En la esquina del campo santo.	In the corner of the holy field.
Gloria al Padre	Glory to the Father
Gloria al Hijo	Glory to the Son
Gloria al Espíritu Santo.	Glory to the Holy Spirit.

(2) The second text was collected in the city of Armenia, a municipality in the department of Sonsonate, in the western zone of El Salvador. The perspective here is that of the deceased child itself:

No me llores madre mía	Don't cry for me, my mother
Ya no llores madre amada	Don't cry any more, beloved mother
Que los ángeles del cielo	May the angels of heaven
Ahí me están esperando.	Be waiting for me.
Ya la esplendida mañana	The splendid morning
Vierte nivea claridad	Pours bright clarity
Anunciando mi llegada	Announcing my arrival
A la patria celestial.	To the heavenly homeland.
Mi padrino y mi madrina	My godfather and my godmother
Me darán palma y corona	They will give me palm and crown
Que el Diosito poderoso	May the almighty God
Les dará su bendición.	Give them his blessing.
A las cuatro de la mañana	At four in the morning
Yo me voy camino al cielo	I'm on my way to heaven
No me llores madre mía	Don't cry for me, my mother
No me llores madre amada.	Don't cry for me, beloved mother.
Despierta madre despierta	Wake up mother, wake up
Mirad que ya amaneció	Look, it's already dawn
Mírame a tus pies postrados	Look at me at your feet
Y dame tu bendición.	And give me your blessing.

(3) The third text is an extensive one, collected in the indigenous town of Panchimalco, in the department of San Salvador. The locals perform this song at least four times each month, because the child

mortality rate is high due to the lack of medical provision in this community:

Yo he venido a esta casa	If I've come to this house
Sin haberme convidado	Without being invited
A cantarle los parabienes	To sing the compliments
A este niño amortajado.	To this shrouded child.
No llores madre amorosa	Do not cry loving mother
No llores sin desconsuelo	Do not cry with grief
Porque tu niño va por el aire	Because your child is going through the air
Sin poder entrar al cielo.	Unable to enter into heaven.
No llores padre querido	Do not cry dear father
No llores sin desatino	Do not cry without nonsense
Porque entre ángeles y serafines	Because between angels and seraphim
Me van abriendo el camino.	They are opening the way for me.
A las cuatro de la mañana	At four in the morning
Sale el ángel para el cielo	The angel leaves for heaven
Con su candela y su guirnalda	With his candle and his garland
Que sus padrinos le dieron.	That his godparents gave him.
A las cuatro de la mañana	At four in the morning
Sale el ángel para el cielo	The angel leaves for heaven
A pedirle a Jesucristo e	To ask Jesus Christ
el perdón de sus padrinos.	The forgiveness of his godparents.
El padrino y la madrina	The godfather and the godmother
merece cetro y corona	Deserve sceptre and crown
porque tienen adelante	Because they have in front of them
una candela en la gloria.	A candle in the glory.
Si porque lo habéis tenido	If because you have had it
te causa tal sentimiento	Causes you such a feeling
déjalo que va a gozar	Let him enjoy
a los reinos de los cielos.	The kingdoms of heaven.
Dios se lo pague a mis padres	God reward it to my parents
por los días que me han criado	For the days that I have been raised
la lechita que me han dado	The milk that I have been given
la Virgen tendrá el cuidado.	The Virgin will take care.
Dios se lo pague a mis padres	God reward it to my parents
por los días que me han criado	For the days that I have been raised
los alimentos que me dieron	The food that they gave me
la Virgen tendrá el cuidado.	The Virgin will take care.
Que dichosos es este niño	How happy is this child
que nació para el cielo	Who was born for heaven

del oriente al poniente	From east to west
la Virgen se lo llevó.	The Virgin took him.
Desde aquí me voy despidiendo	From here I'm saying goodbye
por si no me han conocido	In case you have not met me
Juancito Inocente es mi nombre	Juancito Inocente is my name
Ramírez Pérez mi apelativo.	Ramírez Pérez my last name.
A las tres de la mañana	At three in the morning
Este niño falleció	This child died
Del oriente al poniente	From east to west
La Virgen se lo llevó.	The Virgin took him.
De aquí me voy despidiendo	I'm leaving from here
Florido de este clavel	Flowery of this carnation
Gloria al Padre	Glory to the Father
Gloria al Hijo	Glory to the Son
Gloria al Espíritu Santo.	Glory to the Holy Spirit.
A las dos de la tarde	At two in the afternoon
Me llevaron al cementerio	They took me to the cemetery
Bajo un árbol de naranjo	Under an orange tree
Ahí quedare sepultado.	I will be buried there.
A las dos de la tarde	At two in the afternoon
Me llevaron al cementerio	They took me to the cemetery
Ya mis padres ya se fueron	My parents have already left
Ya se fueron con su reunión.	They left with their meeting.
De aquí me voy despidiendo	I'm leaving from here
De la esquina del camposanto	From the corner of the cemetery
Gloria al Padre	Glory to the Father
Gloria al Hijo	Glory to the Son
Gloria al Espíritu santo.	Glory to the Holy Spirit.
De aquí me voy despidiendo	I'm leaving from here
De la esquina del camposanto	From the corner of the cemetery
Yo he venido a quedarme	I have come to stay
Bajo un árbol de naranjo.	Under an orange tree.

The discovery of a songbook

A musical transcription of these songs has been found in one written source, a compilation made by Francisco Espinosa, member of the National Education Council of El Salvador, who published a songbook titled *Folklore Musical Salvadoreño* in 1949. Here we find the musical transcription 'Los Parabienes', which has been compared with contemporary performances of these songs. Comparative analysis shows how the melody and harmonization have not changed in almost seventy years.[5] However, we were not able to find the text linked to it; our hypothesis is that the compiler made a deliberate decision not to write down the text because different words were found throughout the Salvadorean territory.

* * *

Thanks to this research we have been able to connect with a tradition that links the European and American continents. It is necessary to consider the influence of this type of song and celebration on the cultural development of a given population, since they have served to shape their religious beliefs. Similarly, it has given rise to a new research topic – the origin and purpose of the *Folklore Musical Salvadoreño* songbook – since Salvadorean scholars confirm that there was no previous knowledge of the existence of this book. To conclude this article, we would like to emphasize the importance of safeguarding the musical heritage that the *parabienes*, or *cantos de angelito*, represent, because it is a tradition in danger of extinction.

---

[5] Alejandro Martínez de la Rosa, 'Los parabienes: Tradición, palabra y música para despedir angelitos', *Cuicuilco revista de ciencias antropológicas*, 66 (2016), 108–29.

Jack Riseborough: The Missing Man from the East Norfolk Singing Tradition

CHRIS HEPPA

Jack Riseborough (1886–1948) first came to my attention when I was interviewing Samuel R. Howard of Mautby, Norfolk, about his memories of the singing tradition in the area near Stalham in the north-eastern part of the Norfolk Broads.[1] In this area lived Harry Cox (1885–1971), one of England's best-known and finest traditional singers. Although a younger man, Sam Howard (*b.*1909) actually sang with Harry Cox and his friends, all of whom featured on the seminal *East Anglia Sings* recordings made at the Windmill Inn, Sutton, on 27 October 1947 by the composer and song collector E. J. Moeran for the BBC's Third Programme and broadcast the following month.[2] Yet the very first words Sam had to say to me on the subject of traditional singing in this part of Norfolk were: 'Jack Riseborough – he was a very useful singer.'[3] But this singer from Catfield, a friend of Harry Cox and the others, did not feature in the BBC broadcast. Sometime later, Peter Kennedy mentioned Jack Riseborough in the course of a telephone conversation about the singer John 'Charger' Salmons. I immediately questioned him about Jack, but he could not remember anything about him at that time.

I gradually found out more about Jack Riseborough from Sam Howard and other local people who knew him, in particular from three of his sons, Billy and Eddie Riseborough of Catfield, and George Riseborough of Spa Common, near North Walsham. I learned that his full name was Arthur William John Riseborough, but he was only ever known as Jack. He was a steam-engine driver and engineer, whose occupation involved the threshing of a variety of crops. His father, also called Jack, but not a singer, lived in Sutton, the next

---

[1] Sam Howard was born and originally lived in Potter Heigham, close to the other singers, and had a repertoire of over twenty songs himself. See Christopher Heppa, 'Sam Howard and the East Norfolk Singing Tradition, 1919–1936', in *Folk Song: Tradition, Revival, and Re-Creation*, ed. Ian Russell and David Atkinson (Aberdeen: Elphinstone Institute, University of Aberdeen, 2004), pp. 422–30.
[2] *East Anglia Sings: E. J. Moeran's Legendary 1947 Broadcast*, CD (Musical Traditions SFO 005), which also includes songs from the Eel's Foot, Eastbridge, Suffolk.
[3] Chris Heppa, interview with Sam Howard, Mautby, 11 September 1996.

village north from Catfield, and was also a steam-engine driver and worked on the Sutton windmill, which is the tallest mill in England. At the age of eighty-four, the elder Jack had to be persuaded by his family to come down from the exterior top of the mill where he was oiling the flyer at the back. The nature of the work meant that the younger Jack was often to be seen almost black from the smoke and dirt of the job, and one of his nicknames was 'Black Jack'. A 'sharp' farmer once said to him, 'You're so black you look like a monkey,' to which Jack retorted, 'Yes, and if you play the organ, I'll dance and sing for you.'[4]

Jack was well known as a singer in the area and people who remember his singing all attested to the fact that he was a fine performer, who sang well-known songs like 'The Wild Rover', 'The Apprentice Boy', 'The Crabfish', and 'The Foggy Dew'. His wife, Alice Maud, who came from Fellbrigg, told her sons that when he was young he was a very fine singer indeed. She was a singer herself, who also liked to sing 'The Foggy Dew' and 'The Crabfish'. Like Harry Cox, Jack was keen to learn songs from local singers and it is known that he learned 'The Foggy Dew' from 'Mate' Nudd, a blind singer, who, despite his disability, lived in a houseboat on Hickling Broad. 'Mate' was once ejected from the Pleasure Boat Inn at Hickling because he refused to stop singing his very long version of 'The Barley Mow'.

Jack had nine children, and often went poaching rabbits in order to help feed them. He was accomplished at reading and handwriting, and would teach those skills to anyone who was interested. He was also willing to teach others his songs. He was a noted step-dancer, able to turn on one foot, and was nimble despite his size thirteen boots. He would stand on his head on the table in a pub like the Catherine Wheel in Sutton and step-dance on the ceiling, a practice that was actually quite common among local step-dancers.[5]

He also had a reputation as a hard man, particularly when he was in drink, and he was well known in the area as a prodigious drinker. Harry Cox's son-in-law, Lennie Helsdon, remembered Jack as 'a fighting man, if things weren't going his way'.[6] Although the singing in these Norfolk pubs does not seem to have had a regular 'chairman' (unlike some of the Suffolk singing pubs, such as the well-known Ship at Blaxhall), when necessary Jack was known to call, 'Give order. The

4 Chris Heppa, interview with Billy Riseborough, Catfield, 5 June 1999.
5 Chris Heppa, interview with Eddie Riseborough, Catfield, 9 September 2004.
6 Chris Heppa, interview with Lennie Helsdon, Ludham, 23 July 2003.

singer's on his feet.'[7] He drank and sang largely at the Catherine Wheel or the Windmill in Sutton, occasionally at the Harnser at Stalham Green, and less frequently at the Crown in Catfield.[8]

Jack was friendly with Harry Cox and his singer friends, notably William 'Bullards' Miller of Catfield,[9] Elijah Bell of Sutton, Walter 'Waxy' Gales of Sutton, Charlie Chettleburgh of Sutton, and John 'Charger' Salmons of Stalham Green. Jack had his own nickname, which was 'Fruit', derived from the fact that the Norfolk pronunciation of 'raspberry' is so similar to his surname. The importance of these nicknames is difficult to overstate. George Riseborough told me that when a man called *him* 'Fruit', he knocked him down, saying, 'That's my father's nickname, not mine.'

These Norfolk villages are close together and handy for the local pubs in which the men sang, most notably the Catfield Crown, and the Sutton Windmill and Catherine Wheel. Most singers possessed bicycles, which allowed them to get around a fairly wide area in search of music-making. In fact, popular 'singing pubs' like the Happisburgh Victoria and the Lessingham Star would be so surrounded by bicycles on a Saturday night that it was hard to get inside.[10]

All three of his sons told me not only that E. J. Moeran regularly visited Jack Riseborough, but that Jack was definitely present at the BBC recording session in October 1947. Furthermore, Billy Riseborough believed that Moeran also recorded his father at the Sutton Social Club at Sutton Staithe. By choice, Jack did not possess a wireless, as he thought them noisy and squeaky, though he was a keen listener to gramophone records, in particular recordings made by the popular Irish singer Josef Locke (1917–99), and Jack is known to have sung several of Locke's songs himself. However, the whole Riseborough family gathered around the wireless in a neighbour's house in November 1947 when *East Anglia Sings* was broadcast. They were very disappointed when the programme ended without a performance by their father. They even listened the following week, thinking there might have been another episode. They all knew that Jack had left home to go to the recordings, but he refused to comment when asked why he was not included.

---

[7] Chris Heppa, interview with Herbert 'Harcourt' Warnes, Sutton, 7 April 2005.

[8] Chris Heppa, interview with Eddie Riseborough, Catfield, 9 April 2005.

[9] William Miller has often been referred to as 'Bullets', but many locals called him, quite clearly, 'Bullards'. The two words sound very similar and two of his sons, Les and Jim, were unsure on this point. Bullard's was a popular brand of beer in the area, brewed at the Anchor Brewery, Norwich, until 1967, and recently revived.

[10] Chris Heppa, interview with George Riseborough, Spa Common, 22 May 2018.

I was able to research the BBC Archives for the 1947 broadcast and there is no written mention at all of Jack Riseborough in the programme notes. I was left wondering whether he even turned up that evening. George Riseborough suggested to me, mischievously, that Jack might have gone after 'a bit of skirt' instead. But the Riseborough brothers all agreed that Jack was so proud of his songs that he would definitely have gone. Moreover, a careful listening to the broadcast reveals, I believe, that Jack Riseborough was indeed present. When Charlie Chettleburgh was requested to sing 'The Lost Lady Found', there was some doubt expressed over whether he could sing in view of the fact that he was suffering from a heavy cold. Chettleburgh responded by saying, 'Well, if I can't, *Jack* knows it, or Harry knows it. Harry knows everything.' By 'Harry', of course, he meant Harry Cox, and the only other 'Jacks' present were Riseborough and John Salmons, the latter of whom was generally called 'Charger'. So if Jack Riseborough was indeed present, why was he not recorded? I can tentatively suggest two possible reasons, the second being the more likely.

First, some items in Jack's repertoire might not have been considered by collectors to be 'folk songs' – though, of course, the same could be said of most traditional singers. I have been able to construct a list of his repertoire, which includes many folk songs, Victorian parlour ballads, music hall songs, Josef Locke's Irish songs, and sentimental ditties (see *Appendix*). Everyone who knew him agrees that his favourite song was 'The Black Velvet Band', a song set in Belfast which deals with the betrayal of an innocent man by a pretty woman who is actually a thief, which results in his being transported to Van Diemen's Land (Tasmania) for a street theft that the woman had committed herself. All three of Jack's sons remember visiting a local pub called the Star in the tiny hamlet of Lessingham. They were approached by a local singer called Bert Larter who asked them if they were Jack Riseborough's boys. They replied in the affirmative and Larter responded, 'Blust, your father taught me "The Black Velvet Band".'[11] The story illustrates Jack's readiness to teach songs to others, and the song itself is a popular part of the folk song repertoire.

However, if Jack chose only to sing music hall material or parlour ballads at the recordings, I imagine either that he would not have been recorded or that any recordings made would not have been used. Much more likely, however, is that Moeran and his assistants would have persuaded him to sing to sing something more attuned to their

---

[11] Chris Heppa, interview with George Riseborough, Spa Common, 8 April 2005.

expectations of folk song. If he insisted on material that they considered unsuitable, they could simply omit the recordings later. Moreover, Jack told his son Billy that in fact the only song he sang was 'The Black Velvet Band', which the BBC recordists would surely have found acceptable.

Peter Kennedy told me that when he was working for the BBC in the 1950s recording the folk songs of the British Isles, he was working to a very tight budget and to very strict time constraints. Moeran was presumably working under the same conditions. Singers they visited could be unavailable for any number of reasons – illness, absence from home, being too busy – which meant that days might be wasted, in whole or in part. That is probably why Harry Cox dominated the recordings. All the singers knew a lot of songs, but none as many as Harry, so it would have been convenient for Moeran to get a sprinkling from everyone present, but to rely on Harry Cox for most of the songs. He did actually record other songs by Elijah Bell, Walter Gales, and Charlie Chettleburgh, but they were not included in *East Anglia Sings*.

I strongly suspect that Jack Riseborough was simply too inebriated to sing properly. A meal and drinks were supplied free of charge by the BBC at this session, with the intention of encouraging the singing. That would be like a magnet to a heavy drinker like Jack Riseborough. There was obviously a convivial atmosphere, which can be heard on the recordings, with the singers eager to please and show what they could do, and they all join in the choruses and congratulate one another on their performances.

Jack Riseborough was well known, if not notorious, for his heavy drinking. Les Miller, a son of 'Bullards' and a fine singer himself, described Jack as 'almost an alcoholic'.[12] One story, verified by many people, will illustrate this. One day Jack asked a local farm labourer called Bob 'Sky' Parker, himself notorious as a heavy drinker,[13] if he would like to help him with a Saturday morning's baling at Paston, on the Norfolk coast, and Bob agreed. The steam engine was already fired up the night before, so both men simply had to cycle from their homes and do the work. They were finished around midday, so the two men made their way to the nearby Ship Inn at Paston for a well-earned drink. They proceeded to drink twenty-two pints of mild each, after which Jack suggested a bottle of rum, which they polished off,

---

[12] Chris Heppa, interview with Leslie Miller, Stalham, 14 August 1998.
[13] If anything, Bob 'Sky' Parker was an even heavier drinker than Jack Riseborough (Chris Heppa, interview with Mrs E. Grimes, Stalham Green, 9 April 2005).

half each. Then they cycled back to Catfield, a journey of some eleven miles, with nine more miles for Parker who lived at Fleggburgh. When they parted at a fork in the road, Jack said, 'Very well, Bob, I'll see you tonight at the [Catherine] Wheel at nine o'clock', and apparently they both turned up there as usual.

Jack's sons questioned their father about his non-appearance on the programme, but he refused to give them any explanation. He did tell his son George that he sang only one song, however, and he told his son Billy that this was 'The Black Velvet Band'. Since they all remember Moeran visiting him regularly, it may be that there were recordings, or transcriptions, of his songs made at some point, but none are known to exist. All the singers and the BBC staff present at the Windmill recordings in 1947 are long gone. The youngest person present was Brian Gales, who accompanied his grandfather Walter Gales, the village cobbler from Sutton, possessed of a beautifully sweet, if fragile, voice in spite of his eighty-six years. Brian can be heard shouting 'Well done, granfer' when Walter finishes 'As I Walked Out One Bright May Morning'.

Unfortunately, Brian Gales died prematurely so I never had the chance to ask him about the session. I have interviewed a (then) younger man who was confined with his friends to the other bar of the Windmill while the recordings of the older men were being made, but he was unable to tell me who was present. Jack died of stomach cancer in August 1948, not long after the recording session, and his singing voice had declined rapidly during that last year. When asked why he was going into hospital, Jack replied cheerfully, 'I'm going to have a new firebox fitted!' He was buried in Catfield churchyard, where there is a memorial stone to him and his wife. If drink was the reason why Jack Riseborough was omitted from the BBC recordings, it is a great shame, because so many people I have spoken to over the years have spoken highly of his abilities as a singer.

Jack's son Eddie concurred: 'He might have been a bugger to us, but he was a fine singer.'[14] It is interesting to compare the Riseborough brothers' views on the local traditional singers. George felt that he had not heard enough of the others' performances to compare his father with them, but Eddie thought his father was a far superior singer to Harry Cox. Similarly, Billy considered his father the best of the local singers, along with Walter Gales. Harcourt Warnes told me that Jack's voice was 'higher-pitched' than Harry Cox's. I

---

[14] Chris Heppa, interview with Eddie Riseborough, Catfield, 27 September 2005.

sincerely hope that one day recordings of Jack Riseborough might come to light and then listeners can judge for themselves.

Appendix: Jack Riseborough's known repertoire

Songs that one or more local people remember Jack Riseborough singing include:

- 'The Apprentice Boy' (Roud 263)
- 'The Banks of the Sweet Primroses' (Roud 586)
- 'The Black Velvet Band' (Roud 2146) – Jack's favourite song
- 'The Crabfish' (Roud 149)
- 'The Dark Eyed Sailor' (Roud 265)
- 'Far Away in Australia' (Roud 25792)
- 'The Foggy Dew' (Roud 558)
- 'The Old Rustic Bridge' (Spear and Denhoff, 1881)
- 'The Pretty Ploughboy" (Roud 186) – learned from Harry Cox's 78 rpm record of 1934, which Jack owned and greatly admired
- 'Rock of Ages' (Augustus Toplady, 1763)
- 'The Song of the Thrush' (Roud 1763)
- 'When Your Hair Has Turned to Silver' (P. de Rose/C. Tobias)
- 'Who Rolled the Stone from Dan Murphy's Door?'
- 'The Wild Rover' (Roud 1173).
- also the Josef Locke songs 'When You Were Sweet Sixteen', 'Count Your Blessings', 'Rose of Tralee'.

A. L. Lloyd: Folk Song as Ritual Song

GEORGE HOYLE

A. L. (Bert) Lloyd was born in 1908 and died in 1982, and among other things in a complex, varied, and interesting life he was a key figure in the second English folk song revival during the decades after the Second World War. His main book-length publications are generally acknowledged as having been highly influential in their time, and they still resonate with many on the folk scene, but it could be argued that his more ephemeral articles, and more importantly the sleeve notes he wrote for successive LP releases, especially on the Topic label, have had an equally widespread influence on the way singers and enthusiasts have approached the subject of folk song. Lloyd was closely associated with Topic, which began as the record label of the Workers' Music Association, the musical wing of the Communist Party of Great Britain. An analysis of his views is therefore important for both historical and present-day understanding, and I would like to focus on one particular aspect where his influence is especially clear. Although he was a lifelong Marxist and atheist, he took a particular interest in pagan ritual, shamanism, and folk magic.

My favourite folk record is *Frost and Fire: A Calendar of Ritual and Magic Songs*, the debut album by the Watersons, released on Topic records in 1965.[1] It was *Melody Maker* album of the year and the sleeve notes are by Lloyd. I must admit that I am a Bert Lloyd fan, but I would say that he does sometimes appear to present poetic truths as if they were objective reality. Nevertheless, he is very readable. In the sleeve notes to *Frost and Fire* we find:

> Seasons of anxiety, seasons of joy. The common people had their rites of propitiation and triumph, older than the rituals of the Church and closer bound to their daily lives. This record takes us through a year's calendar, displaying songs that accompanied these ceremonies, season by season.
>
> What are the songs really about? Let's begin with Adam and Eve. The first men plucked their food from bushes and trees, and in open country they become hunters. They learned to tame animals, to grow

---

[1] The Watersons, *Frost and Fire: A Calendar of Ritual and Magic Songs*, LP (Topic 12T136, 1965).

food plants, and turned herdsmen and agriculturists. When plants and beasts abounded, life was good. If they withdrew, people starved. Fertility was vital. Its stream dwindled in winter, ran again in springtime. Gradually, people got the idea of trying to stimulate that fertility by performing stamping dances to waken the earth, leaping dances to provoke crops to grow high and bulls to breed. They tried to bind the potency of nature to themselves, dressing in green leaves or animal skins to perform their magic ceremonies, ritually eating and drinking enormously at certain seasons to take into themselves extra portions of the vital spirit dwelling in sacred animals and plants. Man was on the point of inventing the gods.

The most gifted man in the community took the lead. He was the medicine man, the priest, the king, the representative of divine power. He was the one who dressed in skins or leaves, who killed the sacred animal, cut the sacred tree, led the earth-shaking dances of springtime, lit the reassuring bonfires of midwinter, headed the bands of heroes who marched through the village at critical seasons, singing and dancing for good luck and fine crops, and extracting their rewards for driving off the demons of sterility and want. And because the medicine-man was the representative of all that's fecund, in early times he was killed even before his potency faded so that another vigorous representative could take his place and the continuance of fertility assured. Eventually, as manners softened, the ceremony involving this ritual slaughter, a rite compounded of anxiety, hope and remorse, changed its character. Instead of the king, a slave, a prisoner of war, an animal even was sacrificed, and finally the ceremony became a symbolic spectacle, a pantomime dance of death and resurrection that comprised the first folk play and thus the beginning of all theatre.

When the Christian church arose, it ranged itself against the beliefs and customs of the old nature worship, and prudently annexed many of the seasonal ceremonies. Thus the critical time of the winter solstice, a rich period for pagan ritual, became the season of the Nativity of the new god. The season of the great spring ceremonies became the time of his slaughter and resurrection. So it happens that in many songs on this record, pagan and Christian elements are inextricably tangled. So much is talked of myth and sun worship and such, that it's necessary to recall that behind most of these calendar customs and the songs attached to them lies nothing more mysterious, nothing less realistic, than the yearly round of work carried out in the fields. We've divided our cycle of customs according to the calendar seasons – winter, spring, summer, autumn and winter again. Less formally, we might better have divided them according to the economic seasons – the ploughing, sowing, augmentation and harvesting of crops. For it's due to their relation with economic life, not to any mystical connection, that the song-customs have persisted right up to our own time. Just as one doesn't need to be an ancient Greek to be moved by the plays of Aeschylus, so it's not necessary to be anything other than an ordinary freethinking twentieth century urban western man with a proper regard for humankind, to appreciate the spirit and power of these songs. To our toiling ancestors they meant everything, and in a queer irrational way they can still mean much to us.

From the 1930s, before his interest in folk music became a more dominant part of his life, Lloyd had been interested in myth. He felt that one of the consequences of modern industrial society was the loss of myth as a spiritual and symbolic resource for artists and musicians.

Bert Lloyd's first article on folk song was published in the *Daily Worker* in 1937 under the title 'The People's Own Poetry'.[2] One of the recommended books in the reading list at the end of the article is *The English Ballad: A Short Critical Survey* by Robert Graves, published in 1927, which traces the development of the ballad from its earliest times down to the twentieth century. Included are examples of romantic ballads, sea shanties, and street ballads, as well as a long introductory essay. In 1948, Graves published *The White Goddess: A Historical Grammar of Poetic Myth*, which became a key text for the post-Second World War neo-pagan revival. It is a monumental but contentious work. Folklorists justifiably get exasperated by the factual inaccuracies; many people treasure it as a great poetic work; and for some it is a holy text. It has never been out of print.

In 1938, working for the BBC, Lloyd managed to get the first location recording of folk singing in an East Anglian pub broadcast on the BBC. He described it thus on a later occasion:

> There is in Suffolk, within the sound of a Trinity House foghorn, a remote hamlet reached by narrow, high-hedged, lanes. Among its few cottages and farms is a single inn, The Eel's Foot. To the passer-by this beer house, for that's all it is, is like many another country pub; it's small and undistinguished apart from its curious name. But on Saturday evenings the Eel's Foot is the scene of a dramatic rite which after years of acquaintance is still quite exciting.[3]

The communal session in the Eel's Foot was his first experience of folk music 'in the wild' and the vernacular community ritual he witnessed was formative.

---

[2] *Daily Worker*, 10 February 1937, p. 7.
[3] BBC, *East Anglia Sings*, 19 November 1947.

In 1944, the Workers' Music Association published *The Singing Englishman*, Lloyd's first attempt to synthesize folk song with his Marxist world view. It was a pioneering work and is an easy and entertaining read, but some elements of it will appear somewhat fabulous to the 21st-century reader with over seventy years of subsequent research to draw on. Some of the theories of song origin are obviously inspired by the work of Margaret Murray. Thus Lloyd makes enthusiastic references to a supposedly politically subversive pan-European witch cult, organized into cells or covens, which were 'of course, wildly persecuted and had to work as strictly undercover groups'.[4]

Margaret Murray was the first female lecturer in archaeology at University College London, served as president of the Folklore Society from 1953 to 1955, and is best remembered for her books *The Witch Cult in Western Europe* (1921) and the best-selling *The God of the Witches* (1931) She hypothesized that a Neolithic nature religion survived as an underground cult until at least the late eighteenth century. While generally discredited nowadays, in the 1930s and 1940s it was commonly thought that Margaret Murray's witch-cult theories were credible. She is another key figure in the modern neo-pagan revival and was a great influence on Gerald Gardner, the founder of modern Gardnerian wicca. Gerald Gardner was a member of the Folklore Society from 1939 and briefly on its council in 1946.

Bearing in mind that *The Singing Englishman* was published in 1944 and Gardner's influential *Witchcraft Today* was published in 1951, it is not possible that Gardner's published work influenced Lloyd, and the two men are not reported as having ever met. Lloyd was, however, acquainted with the occultist and ceremonial magician Aleister Crowley at a time when he (Lloyd) was working in the foreign book department of Foyle's bookshop in the early 1930s.[5]

In the accounts I have read of *The Singing Englishman* I have not seen the obvious influence of the work of J. G. Frazer mentioned. I say 'obvious' because Lloyd refers to Frazer directly.[6] Sir James George Frazer is famous for his multi-volume work *The Golden Bough: A Study in Comparative Religion*, the first edition of which was published in 1890. Frazer attempted to define the shared elements of religious

---

[4] A. L. Lloyd, *The Singing Englishman* (London: Workers' Music Association, [1944]), pp. 9–10, 27–28.

[5] Dave Arthur, *Bert: The Life and Times of A. L. Lloyd* (London: Pluto Press, 2012), p. 41.

[6] Lloyd, *Singing Englishman*, p. 9.

belief and scientific thought, discussing fertility rites, human sacrifice, the dying god, the scapegoat, and many other symbols and practices the influence of which could be traced down to the present day. His thesis was that the old religions were fertility cults that revolved around the worship, and periodical sacrifice, of a sacred king. Frazer proposed that humankind progressed from magic through religious belief to scientific thought. The sleeve notes to *Frost and Fire* quoted above show the undoubted influence of Frazer.

In 1958, Lloyd wrote and produced a BBC radio programme called *Musical Pre-History*, a forty-minute look at the music and ceremonials of prehistoric Europe, but I have been unable to locate a recording or transcript. In 1959, *The Penguin Book of English Folk Songs* was published under the editorship of Lloyd and Ralph Vaughan Williams, the president of the EFDSS. In practice, it was essentially Lloyd's work, and it was a hugely influential book. Many revival repertoires have been furnished from it. Lloyd wrote the notes to the songs, and his comments on 'John Barleycorn' are worth citing:

> This ballad is rather a mystery. Is it an unusually coherent folklore survival of the ancient myth of the slain and resurrected Corn-God, or is it the creation of an antiquarian revivalist, which has passed into popular currency and become 'folklorized'? It is in any case an old song, of which an elaborate form was printed in the reign of James I.[7]

This is more measured than his *Frost and Fire* sleeve note on the same song six years later:

> Sometimes called *The Passion of the Corn*. It's such an unusually coherent figuration of the old myth of the Corn-king cut down and rising again, that the sceptical incline to think it may be an invention or refurbishing carried out by some educated antiquarian. If so, he did his work long ago and successfully, for the ballad was already in print in the early years of the seventeenth century.

Which in turn is more measured than his analysis in the 1940s in *The Singing Englishman*:

> Among folksongs whose origins lie in primitive magical religion but few have preserved anything of what they started out with, though just now and then you come across a song supremely beautiful,

---

[7] Ralph Vaughan Williams and A. L. Lloyd (eds), *The Penguin Book of English Folk Songs* (Harmondsworth: Penguin, 1959), p. 116.

supremely dignified and supremely candid, that has kept popular and dignified and even become increasingly so through the periods when all was decadence and the song was taken for a drinking song as happened with 'John Barleycorn', the song of the death and resurrection of the Corn King, who features in magical cults all over the world from the Hebrides to the Himalayas and for all I know beyond.[8]

In 1967, Lloyd made a BBC radio documentary called *Voice of the Gods* which was a study of the sacerdotal voice and an exploration of the use of sound in ritual. That same year, twenty years after *The Singing Englishman*, his seminal *Folk Song in England* was published. Although no less left-leaning in its overall vision, he had dropped some of the controversial statements about witch cults that had appeared in *The Singing Englishman*. The new book was more a history of class struggle:

> The folk songs are lower-class songs specifically in so far as they arise from the common experience of labouring people and express the identity of interest of those people, very often in opposition to the interests of the masters.[9]

For Lloyd, song was not just a personal experience, but a philosophical and political statement. He concluded that a song, in some way, had to form opinion:

> It might be oblique: as for instance in 'Lovely Joan' in which a clever girl upends male superiority and succeeds in extricating herself with aplomb, or even triumph, from an awkward position, or it may be a song that to some extent undermines the conventional mystification of Christianity or bourgeois illusion generally. Songs that tend towards a collective or communal feeling away from an entirely personal navel-gazing one. Songs expressing an attitude either of social responsibility or of irony towards the more illusionistic kinds of institution that our masters try to fob us off with. I like to feel that my audience isn't quite the same when I've finished with them than when I began.[10]

The conclusion that song has to form opinion is telling. Lloyd was a sophisticated communicator. He was a journalist, a folk singer, and a

---

[8] Lloyd, *Singing Englishman* p. 28.
[9] A. L. Lloyd, *Folk Song in England* (London: Lawrence and Wishart, 1967), p. 179.
[10] Arthur, *Bert*, p. 317.

mentor to many performers. He was a highly influential figure, so naturally when some aspect of his work is re-examined it is important that we take notice. I will finish with a great anecdote about Bert Lloyd which came from Mike Waterson at the Lloyd centenary concert held at Cecil Sharp House in 2008:

> Bert was the man who knew everything that I wanted to know about folk music. I remember once I went to hear him give a two-hour-long lecture at Keele Folk Festival and I was awe-inspired by his description of the 'Outlandish Knight', he took it back and back until it ended up as two vases in the British Museum – a thousand years old and I was gobsmacked. Afterwards I sat outside on the steps of the lecture hall and when he came down I said, 'Bert, that was incredible.' He said, 'Michael, in the light of further evidence everything I've said today could be utter bullshit.'[11]

---

[11] Arthur, *Bert*, p. 333

Understanding the Repertoire Choices of Folk Club Singers

PAUL MANSFIELD

The individual and the social

How do amateur folk singers choose what to sing, and which factors are most prominent in their accounts of those choices? Based on fieldwork carried out in 2018, this paper will present singers' views on song characteristics and adaptive behaviour within club environments. The concepts of musical identity and 'optimally distinctive repertoire' are used in discussing the findings. The main message from the research is that song choice occurs in the interaction of individual identity, the content of songs, and performance contexts.

The study was concerned with the experience of singers who perform in folk clubs on an unpaid basis, either as resident club singers or as floor singers. The aim was to gather and analyse the views of a cohort of older singers whose experience connects them to a specific historical stage in England's folk revivals, each singer performing at least a proportion of their repertoire from the traditional folk music canon.

There is an issue of historical documentation here, because a generation of singers connected to the 'second revival' is passing and the form of folk club with which they are associated appears to be in decline and may disappear. The second folk revival is associated with the post-Second World War period, and perhaps particularly the 1960s, when the expansion of folk clubs took place. It has been the subject of some debate in terms of its antecedents and periodization.[1] Nevertheless, the lack of representation of amateur performers' voices is notable: relevant survey or overview studies are dated,[2] while an oral

---

[1] See, for example, Michael Brocken, *The British Folk Revival, 1944–2002* (Aldershot and Burlington, VT: Ashgate, 2003); Georgina Boyes, *The Imagined Village: Culture, Ideology, and the English Folk Revival*, rev. edn (Leeds: No Masters Cooperative, 2010), chapter 8; Trish Winter and Simon Keegan-Phipps, *Performing Englishness: Identity and Politics in a Folk Resurgence* (Manchester: Manchester University Press, 2014), chapter 1.
[2] Ruth Finnegan, *The Hidden Musicians: Music-Making in an English Town* (Cambridge: Cambridge University Press, 1989); Niall MacKinnon, *The British Folk Scene: Musical Performance and Social Identity* (Buckingham: Open University Press, 1993); Brocken, *British Folk Revival*.

history text purporting to cover amateur singers in practice emphasizes the views of professionals.[3]

This study considered both factors that might be deemed to be predominantly individual, and those that present as social factors, such as the influence of the clubs. David Hesmondhalgh refers to music as 'a remarkable meeting point of intimate and social realms',[4] providing a basis for both self-identity and collective identity. Different emphases on the individual and social dimensions can be found in relevant literature, as represented by two contributions in the same edited volume. First, Charles Keil:

> Like your fingerprints, your signature and your voice, your choices of music and the ways you relate to music are plural and are related in a pattern that is all yours, an 'idioculture' or idiosyncratic culture in sound.[5]

Then George Lipsitz, who emphasizes the 'importance of time, place and circumstance in shaping the social meaning of musical practices'.[6] The present study is an example of an empirical investigation that illustrates how the individual and the social dimensions interact in specific contexts.

Method

The study was conducted with seven singers (five male, two female) from the English east midlands, from the smaller towns and villages that lie between the principal cities of Nottingham, Derby, and Leicester. The singers are associated with five different clubs in the area, although four of them sing at the more traditionally oriented clubs within the study, Tigerfolk in Long Eaton, Derbyshire, and Grand Union in Sileby, Leicestershire. The age range of the singers at the time of the research was fifty-five to seventy, with the average towards the upper end of that range.

Interviews were conducted in a lightly structured, conversational manner, giving participants space to develop a narrative about their performance choices in the way they saw fit. Participants were also

---

[3] J. P. Bean, *Singing From the Floor: A History of British Folk Clubs* (London: Faber & Faber, 2014).

[4] David Hesmondhalgh, *Why Music Matters* (Chichester: Wiley Blackwell, 2013), p. 2.

[5] Charles Keil, 'Introduction', in *My Music*, ed. Susan D. Crafts, Daniel Cavicchi, and Charles Keil (Hanover, NH: Wesleyan University Press, 1995), pp. 1–3 (p. 2).

[6] George Lipsitz, 'Foreword', in *My Music*, ed. Susan D. Crafts, Daniel Cavicchi, and Charles Keil (Hanover, NH: Wesleyan University Press, 1995), pp. ix–xix (p. xvi).

asked to fill in diary sheets and took part in a focus group discussion (the quotations from participants cited below are from the interviews unless otherwise indicated). This approach reflects the key pillar in thinking about the research design: the participants are experts in their own experience. It can be acknowledged that the research data is produced jointly by the actions of researcher and participant, and that participants may be led down new avenues of thought during the interview.[7] With any method, however, participants' views may evolve or be articulated in new ways through participation in the research.

With regard to which individuals were approached for the research, the focus was firstly on amateur singers performing folk songs, and secondly on those who by virtue of age and/or experience have a connection to the second folk revival and its organizational expression in the shape of folk clubs. This focus provided clear initial criteria for selection: individuals were approached based on their long-term involvement and their particular roles, such as being regular or resident singers. They may be regarded as core members of the local folk scene.

Choosing songs: words and music, subjects and stories

A striking aspect of the way in which participants went about explaining their choices was the apparent priority given to words, because of either their story-bearing or poetic qualities:

> I think it's always been the same ... song that tells a good story. (Dave S.)

> The combination of words and music has always just fascinated me ... that's why I've liked the Paul Simons, the Dylans, whatever, there are loads of others, people who write a decent song, people who put words to music ... in a way I find moving or whatever, that's what I've liked ... in the tradition, they're words that maybe say something that I think is important, they have evolved from unseen hands and voices, all that sort of stuff. (Colin)

Two of the participants taught English Literature and Drama, so it might be reasonable to assume some iteration between their past employment and leisure pursuits:

---

[7] Robin Legard, Jill Keegan, and Kit Ward, 'In-depth Interviews', in *Qualitative Research Practice: A Guide for Social Science Students and Researchers*, ed. Jane Ritchie and Jane Lewis (London: Sage, 2003), pp. 138–69 (p. 139).

> Poetry is a big thing . . . I taught poetry at A-level . . . Poetry and words are very important, you know? So, yes, the beauty of a particular set of words will capture me. (Jean)

Colin also mentioned the appeal of a single line or image:

> I like some of the quirks in the tradition – I like at the end of 'Dives and Lazarus' where Dives is off to hell to sit upon a serpent's knee, I mean, what's not to like about that image? [laughs]. (Colin)

John, too, commented on the difference that a particular line might make in terms of the attractiveness of a version of a song:

> 'The Golden Vallianty' . . . that's what that version is called, and the thing that first hit me was 'he let the water in and it dazzled in their eyes', and it was just like that one line . . . it's only a small hook, but it's a hook, and I thought, I like that. And there are certain songs that have lines like that . . . they cut through and give the appeal. (John)

One interviewee gave a concise description of the process she went through in evaluating a song, a process that in her case gave more prominence to the appeal of melody:

> A lot of it is based on the music, I like the music first, the tune, and then . . . look at the words and if I like the words as well, then I'll look at it; there's a lot of songs where you like the tune but you think 'I don't like . . . I can't sing that' . . . I have to have some sort of connection . . . sometimes it might be only a single line within the song, which means something to me. (Lyn)

Only one other interviewee offered a view that placed emphasis on the tune:

> There's just something about some tunes, the way that they flow and the distance between the notes that just does something and grabs you and gives you a bit of a shiver when you sing it. (Dave W.)

However, Jean, who frequently mentioned the importance of stories, also talked about the strong appeal of certain tunes. These tunes, of which the principal examples were 'Lovely Joan' and 'Salisbury Plain', appear to be linked to some of her earliest experiences of music – especially the former, which she can recall her grandfather playing on the violin when she was very young. This suggests that very early experiences feed into later choices, perhaps suggesting a role for a subconscious element in decision-making.

John gave examples of the attraction of words, but relied on analogy when it came to music – although this might reflect a wider phenomenon, that people feel confident discussing words but believe that technical knowledge and terminology are required for musical analysis:

> I never analyse things, it's a bit like drinking beer . . . and wines and things, I don't go through this [sniffs] 'Oh yes, there's a nose of this and I can get the aftertaste of that and the other' – if tastes right, if it's to my palette . . . that's what I like. Now, another beer might be in excellent condition, but [winces] no, that's a bit too . . . you know, it doesn't feel right, and very much with music, if it fits, if it settles . . . (John)

The importance of a song's words appears almost universal in the interview accounts, but subject matter is also significant, although most of the participants initially spoke about 'words' before raising 'subject matter'. This might be because the poetic appeal of words has a kind of relative independence from subject matter, or because participants felt that some discrimination in respect of subject matter would be assumed.

It was notable that most of the participants were as clear about what they would not sing as about what they would, and this usually involved song content. Some singers found there were subjects that they had moved away from. John and Dave S. both discussed in some detail the tension between the personal and/or social unacceptability of hunting and the fact that many hunting songs were attractive repertoire items. However, it was not just hunting songs that presented difficulties:

> You think of some of the clubs around, that are rather cosy, would you do some of the more sexually explicit songs or ones that have got a bad word in them, would you get pulled to one side afterwards and be told that wasn't very nice and all that sort of thing? (Dave S.)

> There are a few songs where you might change a word not to offend, or you lose verses: 'Roll the Old Chariot Along', which is something that I will happen to sing once in a while . . . 'a night with the cabin boy' is not the verse you sing these days . . . there are lines you tend to not to go across now. (John)

For Lyn, there were issues to do with gender:

> It seems to me that the majority of folk songs are written from the male point of view . . . while I would sing a third person narrative song about a mining event, I would not sing one where I would be singing as a miner – it stretches the credibility too far for me. (Lyn, post-interview email)

It was noticeable that the issue of sexual violence was almost absent from these discussions. The main exception to this came in an interview with one of the two female respondents who identified the song 'The Two Magicians' as being about rape and hence as unacceptable.

Subject matter was discussed at some length in certain interviews. John mentioned several topics that had attracted his attention, such as calendar customs, songs of place, the lives of men on whaling ships, and other songs of the sea. He also performs themed spots with his wife telling a story and him singing linked songs, so his sense of subject is strong, often involving a historical setting. A contrasting perspective is provided in this quotation:

> I can't see a theme between them [songs on diary sheet] really to be honest, they're just songs that I've heard, and I think, I like that . . . I don't think there is a type of song that I'm more attracted to from a singing point of view it's just, just whether I take to it. (Dave W.)

Participants also gave some indication of their attitude towards including more contemporary material, which again provided some insight into the necessity of lyrical qualities:

> There are some extremely well-written songs about, especially some of the ones that are in the traditional style . . . the words need to be well crafted, so I tend to cringe if the rhymes are a bit too glaringly obvious; if the poem reads like doggerel then I'm probably not going to sing it. (Lyn)

Dave W. had a subject-based example on this topic:

> Being a boater . . . tried to learn some songs from that canal world sort of side of things but I just find them a bit too straightforward . . . they're a bit too worthy and not very interesting to me. Sometimes the words are just too obvious – they tend to be written in sort of very everyday language and there's nothing very clever about the way

they're written, I don't know if that's the right way to describe it? (Dave W.)

This connects back to the relationship between words as poetics and words as subject matter or content, the relative appeal of which might vary. It might be suggested that there are alternative models for ranking the order of importance of each element, with some singers emphasizing words and subject matter (with some individual variation between the importance of those two dimensions) and others being attracted by melody.

However, it soon becomes clear that this approach does not bear much scrutiny, because such rankings do not allow for complexity and variation. Colin has been quoted referring to the appeal of a single image (the serpent's knee), but he also specified preferred subject matter – in fact, he went so far as to say that he could not think of any exceptions to his preferred focus on dignity of labour/social injustice, at least in respect of the traditional part of his repertoire. Similarly, John's highlighting of the line in 'The Golden Vallianty' cannot be used to contend that the poetic qualities of a song override a concern with subject matter; John did say that the appeal of individual lines applies to *certain* songs. Dave W.'s rejection of canal boat songs, holding that the subject matter was attractive but the writing style was not, hints at the potential for additional inquiry at the level of individual songs or song categories.

Lyn's description of the initial appeal of the tune being subject both to evaluation of the acceptability of the words and to the sense of a 'connection' with the content may be important in understanding the complexities of the words–subject–music relationship. However, this description of a process does not capture all that might be said about melody and its potential to act independently of other dimensions of a song. As noted above, singers may say less about this aspect of their repertoire because they feel they lack the right vocabulary to describe musical characteristics.

Becoming a performer and adjusting to the club setting

The interviews provided clear evidence of biographical influences on performer identity, often revealing quite different levels and types of early experiences, including singing in non-folk music contexts:

Because of the background I'd always performed – I did my first solo, so I'm told, at the age of two...at a Sunday School anniversary ... right through my childhood I would do it. (Lyn)

> I did get quite a lot of experience in performance, including solo performance . . . but in classical music. (Jean)

John is an example of a singer who began singing in clubs as a teenager apparently without any lack of self-confidence:

> When you're that age, you're sort of full of confidence, you know, and you know everything and, you know, 'of course I can do it'. (John)

In contrast, Dave W. did not attempt singing in a club until he had had long experience of joining in morris dancers' singarounds:

> Even just singing to a group of friends, it's quite a mental step to get over, to make that first public performance really, even though it's with friends. (Dave W.)

The idea that there were no confidence issues for those who had proved competent in classical music at school – and the contrary argument that those lacking that sort of experience inevitably lacked confidence – is too simplistic. John and Dave S. are good examples of singers who referred neither to accomplishments in school music nor to any lack of confidence.

Confidence is a concept that also links to the performer–audience relationship and how that in turn adapts to a club environment, as per Dave W.'s description of audience participation as a form of support for a singer:

> When you're starting singing more publicly you're very nervous, it's great to sing songs everyone else can join in the chorus really, it gives you that extra bit of confidence to get you back on track if you've wobbled off tune or if you've forgotten the words, it just gets you back into the swing of it again. (Dave W.).

Dave S. was aware of this dimension through the unusual debut performing experience of singing as part of a booked duo rather than as a floor-spot soloist:

> It was our first booking and it also turned out to be our last booking . . . the thing when we were thrown off the stage, the thing was we weren't holding the crowd, so sometimes you know when this is happening, it's all down to experience. (Dave S.)

Lyn's approach also changed at a time when she was performing as half of a semi-professional duo: 'you become more audience-orientated ... you become more aware of that you're there to entertain'. These examples suggest that choices may involve making use of past experiences and seeking to maximize a positive response or avoid a negative outcome (in the form of unfavourable audience response).

John and Dave W. added further reflections on the audience and on performer confidence:

> [As a novice performer] you're probably hypersensitive to [mimes audience sighing and coughing] ... but also if people join in, or respond if you say something, and it depends on the warmth of the applause at the end. (John, focus group)

> If you were talking in a meeting or something and you find that people just look as if they're not paying attention, you know, looking at their phone or whatever, it's the same with singing really ... I enjoy singing to myself [laughs] but if I'm singing in front of an audience I'd like to know that they're listening to me. (Dave W.)

A further dimension of adjusting to the club environment is the singer's perception of what kind of repertoire is acceptable at a particular club. The studies by MacKinnon and Finnegan point to substantial diversity within the folk scene, providing a basis for some degree of individual choice. MacKinnon comments that genre expectations in performance are 'commonly broken', [8] and Finnegan found it difficult to define the limits of the music she witnessed being performed: 'It varied not only between different groups and clubs, but even at the same clubs on different nights; and it was not fully agreed where the boundaries of "folk" should be drawn.'[9]

However, some clubs have had an historic emphasis on a specific repertoire. An example of this is the now-defunct Nottingham Traditional Music Club (NTMC), of which the present-day Tigerfolk club at Long Eaton was originally an offshoot, which was certainly perceived as having a strict policy:

> You did get scowled at if you sang the wrong sort of song [at NTMC] and you weren't asked to sing another time; it was made fairly obvious. (Lyn, focus group)

---

[8] MacKinnon, *British Folk Scene*, p. 55.
[9] Finnegan, *Hidden Musicians*, p. 65.

Lyn's comment is a rare example of the use of a kind of sanction in enforcing club norms. Other interview evidence that confirmed that singers were aware of the differences between clubs included the following:

> I do tend to adjust what I'm singing on a particular occasion, to the place that I'm singing it, so the Tiger folk club for example I'll try to pick something from the more traditional end of my repertoire . . . Poppy folk club – you can sing almost anything there. (Dave W.)

> I've not been to the Tiger, but they're pretty trad over there, aren't they? So I know that, so I wouldn't go with . . . I mean, I have enough trad songs in my repertoire to make sure I had two or three I was thinking of doing. (Colin)

However, not every singer in the study felt the need to make adjustments of this sort:

> When I sing in a folk club, to be honest, I'm singing for me, I'm not singing for the audience, I'll sing because I enjoy singing, and the audience is incidental. (Bill, focus group)

> I tend to learn the song for the sake of the song – and then I'll just sing it wherever I go. (Jean)

Participants also reported the ability to vary from what they planned to sing, which is an attribute that relates both to performer confidence and to sensitive appreciation of the requirements of the situation, both of which may develop over time. Nearly every interviewee gave an example of this and it was further evidenced in participants' diary sheets. Lyn's contribution is typical:

> You might have planned to sing a gentle quiet love song, and the person before you sings a gentle quiet love song . . . so, OK [laughs], not a good idea to follow that with another one, we'll do something different, or sometimes singarounds can get a bit dark, it can be full of death and destruction and things like that, so you try to find something that's a bit more light-hearted. (Lyn)

If we compare the comments made in the interviews with the evidence from participants' diary sheets, a distinction might be observed between normative influences based on the characteristics of the relevant clubs, and situational effects which might be more heterogeneous. Consideration of the four most common reasons for choices of song given in the diary entries illustrates this point. The single most frequent reason was responding to a theme – both in the sense that the performance event had a themed approach (club norm effect), and in the sense of responding to an emergent theme in a particular club night (situational effect). However, the prominence of this factor might have resulted from three of the singers having attended an afternoon singaround in Leicestershire that used a themed approach, something not typical of the evening folk clubs in the study.

The placing of chorus songs at the beginning or the end of the evening was also frequently mentioned, and may be considered a product of club norms. However, the other two common categories were, first, trying out a new song or reinforcing a recently learned one; and second, singing a song that linked to the season or the current weather. These appear to be less determined by club characteristics. There were some explicit references to such influences, such as Jean's note 'Grand Union likes choruses', but the evidence of the diary sheets seems to suggest that choices arose from a wider range of reasons than the nature of the club alone.

Distinctiveness of repertoire

One theory that might be tested or evidenced in studies of individual repertoire is that of 'optimal distinctiveness'. Greenberg and Rentfrow explain:

> According to this perspective, individuals have conflicting needs for similarity and uniqueness – too much similarity is insufficiently self-defining but too much uniqueness is isolating – so they strive to attain an optimal level of distinctiveness.[10]

There were indications that singers were aware of distinctiveness as a positive value:

> I sing perhaps a little more obscure songs at Tiger because I don't want to find myself singing something that somebody's already sung. (Lyn)

> I do look for different versions – because it's a poor bloody state of affairs if everybody . . . if every Indian restaurant you went to you

---

[10] David M. Greenberg and Peter J. Rentfrow, 'The Social Psychological Underpinnings of Musical Identities', in *The Oxford Handbook of Music Identities*, ed. Raymond MacDonald, David J. Hargreaves, and Dorothy Miell (Oxford: Oxford University Press, 2017), pp. 304–32 (p. 306).

could only get a beef Madras or a lamb korma or something. (John, focus group)

Jean provided two different reasons for having a distinctive repertoire:

I quite often loved songs that no one else was singing . . . and what I chose to sing in clubs right from the beginning was the songs that I wanted to hear sung, but no one else was singing them. (Jean, interview)

I've deliberately gone to sing songs I didn't think anyone else would be singing – that was actually a lack of confidence in some ways, I just wanted to make sure that whatever I sang, people would want to listen to the song because the song would be different. (Jean, focus group)

It is not unusual for floor singers to have one or two 'novelty' numbers from outside the normal folk repertoire, but that type of distinctiveness was almost absent from the study sample. Colin was the only participant to offer an example, which included a reference to planned distinctiveness of repertoire:

I don't know if you've heard me do 'Champion the Wonder Horse' with my banjo, but it just works, and it also fits my own criteria 'this'll make 'em go "what?"'. But I think it works nicely as a hillbilly song almost. (Colin)

Evolution of repertoire

Song choices may be linked to the evolution of a performance career, as is suggested by this account of beginning to perform in the mid-1960s:

Within a few months sea shanties were the big thing . . . [then] the ballads started to chip away at me a bit . . . political songs were also a big thing. Certainly in the early stages though it was the shanties and drifting into the ballads. (Dave S.)

Dave S. added that when he first moved to the east midlands from his native north-east he found that there was a high level of interest in the regional songs he brought with him, so that repertoire provided the basis for his first year of performing in the new area. This is an example of repertoire not being changed by the club environment or audience reaction but being reinforced by it – perhaps unexpectedly so, in the sense that repertoire from another part of the country might not be guaranteed a positive reception.

The idea that a repertoire is something that is consciously constructed was explicitly rejected in one contribution to the group discussion:

> Didn't build a repertoire in the sense of putting together something that I thought was a repertoire, it was just 'that's a good song, I'll sing that now', and it goes into the book, you know. (Bill, focus group)

In other focus group comments, Lyn argued that the time-expense of researching new songs might make it likely that a singer would 'stick with your existing repertoire or learn songs you hear from other people', while Jean suggested that occasional new material was necessary to 'keep in the practice of learning'. John referred to the frequency of performing: 'It depends how much singing you do ... maybe the pressure [to learn new songs] isn't on when you don't sing so much.'

This is clearly related to the availability of local clubs: two of the five clubs meet monthly, one twice a month, and the other every two weeks. Thus becoming a regular performer at one club rather than another is likely to have implications for repertoire size and variety. However, Bill pointed out that some singers might feel safer with a repertoire they had acquired in the distant past, rather than trying new material, irrespective of the frequency of performing:

> There are people who when they stand up you know exactly what you're going to get from them, and they'll never change it ... they've never experimented and perhaps they don't feel confident to experiment. (Bill, focus group)

Another way in which the factor of time presented in the study data was in relation to the performer's confidence:

> I sort of pick up songs and learn them just because I like them and I think, more so now, because it suits my voice – I feel much more confident now that it's going to come out right from the first ... I don't know that's changed *what* I sing ... it might have given me a bit more confidence to sing those solo [non-chorus] songs. (Dave W.)

Ideas of performance career and repertoire evolution were not the specific focus of the study, but the research findings suggest this could be an area for further investigation.

Revisiting the individual and the social

Clearly, settings in which to perform must be available in order for singers to become established as performers and to stay in that role over an extended period. The clubs need to appeal to, welcome, and retain individual performers; clubs may also close or re-form, and change or evolve their musical policies, so the availability of performance settings cannot be taken for granted. In this study, most of the participants had experienced major relocations within the UK in earlier adulthood. They would have had to investigate whether clubs were available in their new locations, whether those clubs were attractive to attend, and whether they would accept the singers' habitual repertoire preferences (and whether, as singers, they were prepared to change). For long-standing performers, much of this will have been in the relatively distant past, and it is possible to imagine tracking the choices of younger singers as they first engage with clubs in order to provide a fuller picture. Investigating early musical experiences may help us to understand both what attracted people to folk music in the first place, and identify features, such as an interest in the words, that are still present in their later performance choices.

Participants were aware of differences between clubs, but not all indicated that club norms were a particularly strong influence. This might be partly due to their length of involvement with the clubs and also the broader effects of being experienced as a performer. Analysis of the diary sheets provided a different angle, the distinction between normative and other situational influences. It proved helpful to use the three different methods – interviews, diary sheets, and a focus group – because they produced different insights into the mixture of individual and social factors.

It was noticeable that, apart from indirectly through an awareness of differences between clubs, there was little explicit concern with issues of genre boundaries or canonical repertoire. In effect, what was apparent was the bottom-up making of repertoire, produced by the interaction of the individual and the performance environment. This seems to be the case even though individuals (and indeed clubs) will have been influenced, whether recently or in the relatively distant past, by broader ideas in circulation about the nature of folk music. The evidence of the study suggests that for some, perhaps most, performers the type of song performed is largely consistent with their own early interests – although there may be more to learn about the relationship between initial experiences, repertoire formation, and later development. Ideas from the literature about musical education and the development of careers in other music genres might be usefully employed in the folk music context.[11]

While themes such as conformity and adjustment were reflected to a certain extent, other psychological ideas, such as learning from past experiences, were more clearly present in participants' accounts. The concepts of competence and confidence also arose in response to the focus on performing in the interviews. Confidence may be viewed as one connecting point between the individual and the social. A singer might have what they consider a strong repertoire, and they might have somewhere to perform it, but they need to be confident about performing in that environment. To illustrate this, a question that a singer might ask him-/herself is: 'I like this song and I know I can sing it, but do I feel confident to sing this song *here?*' This in turn will connect to earlier experiences and the issue of validation.

The clubs where people perform might reinforce an individual approach to repertoire, or they might influence choice, strongly or weakly. Despite the strength of socialization effects not presenting consistently across the study sample, the suggestion that what is most important about musical choices is their individual uniqueness,[12] is not supported by the evidence of this study. Rather, it may be argued that a more accurate description is the idea of repertoire as a dynamic phenomenon existing in a social context.[13] Similarly, writers on the topic of musical identity tend to emphasize the interplay of the individual and social. Elliott and Silverman, for example, refer to factors that are '*socially situated* and co-constructed through continuous engagements' (original emphasis).[14]

This study has established that there are common characteristics of folk songs that are cited consistently by amateur folk singers when they are asked to explain their repertoire choices; the relative weight of each influence, however, differs between individuals and so variation based in biography merits consideration. The other key point is that complexity at the level of the individual should be considered alongside, and as something intermixed with, a similarly variable

---

[11] See, for example, Jackie Wiggins, 'Vulnerability and Agency in Being and Becoming a Musician', *Music Education Research*, 13 (2011), 355–67.

[12] Keil, 'Introduction', p. 2.

[13] Tia DeNora, *Music in Everyday Life* (Cambridge: Cambridge University Press, 2000), p. 6.

[14] David J. Elliott and Marissa Silverman, 'Identities and Music: Reclaiming Personhood', in *The Oxford Handbook of Music Identities*, ed. Raymond MacDonald, David J. Hargreaves, and Dorothy Miell (Oxford: Oxford University Press, 2017), pp. 27–45 (p. 31).

picture of how the singer interacts with their local club(s). A model using three dimensions represents the range of interacting factors that the study identified:

- Repertoire: subject matter, lyrical attributes, melody
- Performer identity: extent of experience, performance in other genres, confidence
- Club environment: range of normative repertoire, opportunity to perform/frequency, audience response.

The study aimed to document the views and experiences of a cohort of older singers performing in club environments which relate to an historically significant stage in England's folk revivals. If those environments decline, disappear, or merely change, consideration of both the individual and social aspects of personal repertoires will nonetheless remain relevant to the study of folk singing in whatever new performance settings might emerge.

National Airs in Georgian Libraries

KAREN E. McAULAY

Many libraries are proud to boast a wide variety of very old folk song scores among their special collections. The routes on to those library shelves are more varied than one might imagine – music may have been purchased new or second-hand, gifted by a benefactor or their descendants, or even acquired from another library. However, for nine British libraries in the eighteenth and early nineteenth centuries, and two Irish libraries from 1800 onwards there was another route, enshrined in law: legal deposit. The libraries in question were:

Aberdeen University Library
Cambridge University Library
Dublin, King's Inns Library (after 1801)
Edinburgh, Advocates Library
Edinburgh University Library
Glasgow University Library
London, British Museum (now the British Library)
London, Sion College Library
Oxford, Bodleian Library,
St Andrews University Library
Trinity College Dublin (after 1801).

The traditional songbooks that ended up in these libraries are just a tiny subset of all the publications that followed this route. Each library's story is unique, but in the present paper I shall focus on musical scores in two particular libraries in order to share what we know about the early library users and custodians, and why these collections are so significant.

Strictly speaking, all British publications were meant to be registered with the Company of Stationers at Stationers' Hall, although it is far from clear that this was always carried out. Legislation enacted in Queen Anne's time then introduced a period of copyright protection and also required the legal deposit of copies in designated libraries. Music was included from the outset, although it took legal challenges in the 1780s before it was finally clarified that music, despite being engraved rather than typeset, was entitled to the same protection as books.

By 1836, the whole process had come to be resented by publishers and was causing considerable frustration to the university libraries – resented because publishers objected to supplying free books to so many libraries, and frustrating for the university libraries because they were struggling to get their legal entitlement. Moreover, the university libraries really only wanted the kind of books that would be useful to their scholars, but the legislation entitled them to everything that was printed, from ladies' diaries to commercial labels, school books to music scores. Music was not a university subject at that time, so in one sense it was barely a step away from being considered ephemeral. However, the legislation entitled the libraries to music, and a flourishing music publishing trade meant a lot of music.

In the early nineteenth century, in response to complaints from the publishers, an official commission set out to find out how the legal deposit system was working. Eventually, in 1836, the Library Deposit Act stripped most of the universities of their entitlement and library book grants were implemented instead. The universities that lost their entitlement now had the opportunity to buy the books they needed. Nowadays, publishers are required by law to provide legal deposit copies to the British Library and just a few other national and university libraries:

British Library
Bodleian Library
Cambridge University Library
National Library of Scotland (Edinburgh)
National Library of Wales (Aberystwyth)
Trinity College Dublin.

The British Library automatically receives everything; the others have formally to request items.

My research interest into the historical legal deposit collections began some three years ago, through a contact at the University of St Andrews. After reading Elizabeth Frame's article about the four hundred-plus bound volumes that make up the Library's Copyright Music Collection, it was clear that this material merited further exploration.[1] Most of the volumes were bound compilations of single pieces of sheet music, with just a few fatter volumes where, in the early nineteenth century, someone had taken some care to collate

---

[1] Elizabeth Ann Frame, 'The Copyright Collection of Music in the University Library, St Andrews: A Brief Account', *Edinburgh Bibliographical Society Transactions*, 5.4 (1985), 1–9.

piano music, songs, instrumental music, and so on into workable volumes.

There was also a lot of documentation about the collection, along with a handwritten catalogue made around 1826 by a professor's niece called Miss Lambert, and thousands of pages of loan registers. I transcribed half a century of music loan data, from 1801, when the music began to be bound into workable volumes, up until 1849. By that date even the most up-to-date legal deposit music was thirteen years old, and much was of the kind that would quite quickly go out of fashion. Music loans were already dwindling fast, making a close search far less fruitful.

Between 1801 and 1849, the university's professors and students borrowed music for their own use, and presumably also for family members. Professors could also borrow books and music for their friends, who included a broad cross-section of the town and country's music-lovers, including clergymen and retired military men, and married and unmarried ladies. Unmarried ladies – perhaps very young women – borrowed more than married women during the first couple of decades, but then the pendulum swung the other way. Maybe there were societal changes, or perhaps some of the young women had married and were now borrowing under their new names.

Libraries did not always request everything that had been registered at Stationers' Hall. Neither did they keep everything, particularly the ephemeral material. One would imagine that sheet music was low down the list of priorities. The University of St Andrews library committee regularly inspected the latest consignment from London, putting materials into different categories which would be dealt with in order of priority, and bundling up the least significant materials. Despite this, the university kept an enormous amount of music, beginning to bind it in large folio volumes from 1801 onwards. It was certainly appreciated by local music-lovers. For example, Alexander Campbell published the first book of his *Albyn's Anthology* in 1816. It was logged as having been received at St Andrews in June 1817, was borrowed once before it even went for binding, and was then bound with two other national song scores, by 1821 at the latest.

Much of the legal deposit music at St Andrews is now catalogued online, although some of the earlier material remains unlisted except in Miss Lambert's catalogue notebooks of 1826.[2] Looking through those notebooks, it was clear that a lot of Scottish material was kept –

---

[2] Miss Lambert received a very small payment in 1826, but the catalogues were added to (not necessarily entirely by her) until the collection reached its natural end in 1836.

perhaps even more Scottish-*influenced* music, such as Scottish themes and variations, than music actually originating from Scottish publishers. Interestingly, there were more Scottish songs than Scottish fiddle tune collections. To understand why this might be, one needs to know a little more about the registers at Stationers' Hall, so let us briefly outline the facts.

It is possible to go and inspect the registers at Stationers' Hall, but they were microfilmed some years ago and a few libraries do hold sets of the microfilms. Additionally, an online package of digital images of the registers has recently been published, although it is beyond the means of most libraries. However, a useful book edited by Michael Kassler lists all music registered at Stationers' Hall in the period 1710–1818.[3] The last eighteen years of Kassler's inventory come from a slightly different source and a few pieces may not be listed (*Albyn's Anthology* is missing, for a start); there is less bibliographical detail in this section but it is still very useful. The bibliography stops at 1818 and there is currently no published listing covering music from the period 1819–36, after which legal deposit arrangements changed.

It is interesting to note that, even allowing for the fact that only a small percentage of publishers actually obeyed the law and registered their books and music, very few fiddle tune books were registered at all, so they would not have made their way into the legal deposit collections via the usual route. An earlier AHRC-funded research project, the Bass Culture project, confirmed that very many fiddle tune books for social dancing were published in Scotland during the late eighteenth and early nineteenth centuries,[4] and nearly all of them had something like 'Entered at Stationers' Hall' clearly printed on the title page. So why were they not registered?

Nancy Mace suggests that publishers only registered books they thought likely to need copyright protection.[5] It is also a commonly held assumption that the magic words 'Entered at Stationers' Hall' were printed as a deterrent, even when the title was not registered. Why else would Niel and Nathaniel Gow's collections have the phrase printed on the title page, while only a minority of them actually appear in Kassler's Stationers' Hall listing?

---

[3] Michael Kassler, *Music Entries at Stationers' Hall, 1710–1818, from Lists Prepared for William Hawes, D. W. Krummel, and Alan Tyson, and from Other Sources* (Aldershot and Burlington, VT: Ashgate, 2004).

[4] http://hms.scot/.

[5] Nancy A. Mace, 'The Market for Music in the Late Eighteenth Century and the Entry Books of the Stationers' Company', *The Library*, 7th ser., 2 (2009), 157–87.

At any rate, not many Scottish fiddle tune collections were registered, and this might explain why hardly any made their way into the St Andrews Copyright Music Collection. Interestingly enough, the quadrille, an early nineteenth-century arrival on the dance scene which may have been published in greater quantities for use all over Britain, is well represented in the collection.

Compared with the more purely functional Scottish fiddle tune collections, national song collections were very popular in many drawing rooms, and their use crossed national and class boundaries. The Edinburgh publisher George Thomson's lavish Scottish song collections transformed traditional songs into art music. With words by Robert Burns and musical arrangements by leading composers of the day (Haydn, Beethoven, and the now-forgotten Kozeluch), they are nonetheless probably unknown to many of today's traditional musicians. The scores come complete with violin and cello lines, intricate introductions and codas, and optional separate parts for the instrumentalists. Even at the time of writing, Thomson complained to Beethoven that his settings were too difficult for the young ladies of Edinburgh, while Burns objected to having to write anglicized texts. They are beautifully crafted art songs in their own right, but in an unfamiliar idiom: high art music of their time, often with complex harmonies that disregard the original modality. These books flew off the shelves in Georgian St Andrews, as did Thomson's Welsh and Irish collections. Moore's *Irish Melodies* were also popular, both as poems and in musical settings by Stevenson and Bishop. There was also enthusiasm for the exoticism implied by Byron's *Hebrew Melodies* and their musical settings by Isaac Nathan.[6]

Albyn's Anthology, mentioned above, can also be singled out. It is an important collection containing Highland, Lowland, and Borders tunes. Alexander Campbell made two tours to collect tunes, one to the Highlands and Islands in 1815, publishing his first book the following year. He subsequently made a shorter trip to the Borders, resulting in a second volume which was published in 1818. He was arguably one of Scotland's first ethnomusicologists. The words were an assortment of old and newly written verses, some in Gaelic, some written by Campbell himself, and others by James Hogg and Walter Scott. Campbell displayed little flair at writing piano accompaniments and struggled to deal with modalities other than major/minor. To this day, the collection is regularly referenced, but it is doubtful whether anyone performs the tunes with the accompaniments that Campbell

---

[6] There was very little genuinely authentic Jewish music amongst them.

provided. It does, however, provide good source material for making new arrangements.

The St Andrews copy of *Albyn's Anthology*, volume 1, was bound with two other books to make up volume 296 of the Copyright Music Collection. These were Thomson's *Scottish Airs*, volume 5, and his *Welsh Airs*, volume 3, which probably accounts for the volume's popularity with borrowers. Over the period 1821–49 it was borrowed fifteen times by professors, twice more by their friends, and once by an unmarried lady. Obviously, we do not know who used the music once a professor had taken it home – it could have been for family use. Today, however, the bound volume contains just the Welsh airs – there is no trace of the others. Never make the mistake of assuming that things in libraries do not fall apart, get lost, moved about, re-bound, or some combination of these. Furthermore, there is no evidence at all that St Andrews ever had the second volume of *Albyn's Anthology*.

The extent of the St Andrews Copyright Music Collection, allied with its supplementary archival documentation, makes it rather special and worthy of particular attention. After analysing the borrowing records, and investigating some of the names that cropped up, I was subsequently awarded AHRC network funding to investigate what had happened to the whole of the British/UK Georgian legal deposit music collections; the network is called 'Claimed from Stationers' Hall', reflecting the origin of the collections.

Looking at the national scene, however, it is evident that there is no one-size-fits-all pattern. The British Library's collection is the most complete and is all catalogued online. When legal deposit first started, the library was the Royal Library, which then became the British Museum Library, and finally the British Library. As a reference library, the books were never borrowed, but anything that was registered under legal deposit is available for consultation by following the correct procedures for registering as a reader. Kassler's inventory gives the British Library shelfmark for most of the items listed, or occasionally a shelfmark in another library for the rare occasions when an item could not be traced in the British Library.

Oxford's Bodleian Library and Glasgow University Library have excellent collections, the vast majority catalogued online. However, Cambridge University Library, which may have almost as many holdings, does not have everything listed online. The National Library of Scotland, which started life as the Advocates Library in Edinburgh, has a paper-slip catalogue accessible only by appointment or by making a reference request. It is also hard to tell what music arrived there by legal deposit. Music in the early nineteenth-century Advocates Library is actually documented as having been somewhat disorganized.[7]

Some libraries were discerning about what they kept. Oxford and Cambridge responded to the parliamentary commission with a list of items that they had chosen not to keep. Some of their exclusions will surprise the modern reader, such as novels by Jane Austen and a piece by Beethoven. Cambridge University Library rejected *Albyn's Anthology* and a collection by Alexander Campbell's rival, Simon Fraser, whose *Highland Airs* also appeared in 1816, not to mention works by the west of Scotland's renowned poet, Robert Tannahill. Meanwhile, Aberdeen and Edinburgh universities certainly sold some music, and the other London library, the theological Sion College, sold stock when it fell on hard times, later transferring anything of value, which includes very little music, to Lambeth Palace.

Most recently, I have been examining legal deposit music at the University of Edinburgh and making some unexpected discoveries. Edinburgh has had an endowment providing for a Professor of Music since the mid-nineteenth century, although formal lectures did not start until later on. The Reid Music School, endowed by General Reid, had its own library, which in 1939 was reorganized and catalogued by Hans Gál, an exiled German musicologist.[8] The preface to Gál's published catalogue makes some quite disparaging remarks about British music of the Georgian era, and he did not index every single popular song in the collection. Again, it is difficult to make positive identifications of much legal deposit music; this involves comparing binding styles and looking for book stamps that either mention Stationers' Hall or indicate early arrival into the library collection.

However, there is a certain fascination in trying to establish why particular pieces of music might have been retained by the University of Edinburgh when so much no longer survives. Whoever curated this collection in earlier times seems to have favoured certain categories of music, such as pedagogical material – manuals on how to improvise accompaniments over a figured bass, for example. Maybe these survived because they had an obvious value for teaching music theory. Another category is items commemorating events of national

---

[7] Edinburgh, National Library of Scotland, FR.339.3/51, loose papers concerning the Advocates Library.

[8] Hans Gál, *Catalogue of Manuscripts, Printed Music and Books on Music up to 1850 in the Library of the Music Department at the University of Edinburgh (Reid Library)* (Edinburgh: Oliver and Boyd, 1941).

significance. There are piano pieces to commemorate Napoleonic battles, complete with drum rolls and fanfares (Gál despised these), and anthems composed to mark the deaths of Charlotte Augusta, Princess of Wales, who died in 1817, and her grandmother, Queen Charlotte, wife of George III, the following year.

Of particular interest to students and researchers of folk song today are the Georgian collections of national songs, which reveal an interpretation of 'national songs' that is rather different from our modern definition. It seems clear that, whether via legal deposit or otherwise, the curators of the Reid music collection made a point of keeping collections of this kind. For example, Kitchiner's *The Loyal and National Songs of England*, and its partner volume, *The Sea Songs of England*, published together in 1823, definitely arrived via legal deposit. Plainly judged significant at the time, these collections are also held by several other legal deposit libraries. Their contents are national in the sense of being patriotic, but they are certainly not traditional songs. Rather, they comprise songs by British composers such as Blow, Morley, Purcell, Croft, Arne, and Dibdin, and include 'God Save the King' and 'Rule, Britannia'. Published two years after George IV's coronation and dedicated to the monarch, Kitchiner provided a lavish title page, the top engraving of which is an exact copy of a coronation ticket to Westminster Hall, the only changed details being the addition of the words 'Loyal and National' and 'Songs of England' in place of the ticket numbers (*Figure 1*). The combination of a new edition of national songs and the commemoration of a significant national event must have appealed to whoever was curating music at the time. Sadly, the collection was not well reviewed when it appeared. *The Harmonicon*, for example, praised Kitchiner for his patriotism rather than his musical knowledge.

Although early nineteenth-century national songs are not often performed today, it is fascinating to trace how repertoires have changed and developed, and to consider the revealing introductions which set these collections in context. Those more founded on folk music focus strongly on authenticity and origins.[9] Kitchiner's art song collection, however, is far from alone in displaying its patriotism for a country that had proved victorious in the Napoleonic Wars and

---

[9] While the present article has focused on song, it should be noted that prefaces, introductions, and even apparently insignificant footnotes are every bit as noteworthy in fiddle tune collections. One has only to look at the Gow collections of Scottish dance tunes, for example, to find a wealth of detail about their views on authenticity and tune provenance.

extended its global influence. Moreover, the oft-expressed idea that England had no national music was like a red rag to a bull. Kitchiner was at pains to stress:

> while the Welsh, Scotch and Irish Airs and Songs have been collected and preserved, – those of England have been so much neglected! – that some have even said, 'the English have no National Songs'. The MUSICIANS OF ENGLAND, have been equal to her POETS! and not inferior to those of any Country. This first Number [will prove] no Nation in the World has half so many Loyal, nor half so many National Songs.[10]

Figure 1
Wm. Kitchiner's *Loyal and National Songs of England*.

---

[10] William Kitchiner, *The Loyal and National Songs of England, for One, Two, and Three Voices* (London: printed for Hurst, Robinson, and Co., 1823), p. 3.

English compilers naturally defended their own country's song legacy, but compilers from other countries took a rather different view of England's heritage. Thomas Moore's *A Selection of Popular National Airs* of 1818 is also held in Edinburgh University Library.[11] Moore's opening advertisement takes a directly opposite line from Kitchiner:

> It is Cicero, I believe, who says 'natura ad modos ducimur'; and the abundance of wild, indigenous airs, which almost every country, except England, possesses, sufficiently proves the truth of this assertion.

Bound with Moore's *Selection of Popular National Airs*, I found Charles, Baron Arnim's marginally earlier *A Selection of German National Melodies* (1814–16) and another book of the same era called *The Russian Troubadour*.[12] Arnim supplies a whole Dissertation 'On National Music' and displays a similar attitude to Moore's:

> England may perhaps be said not to possess any national music at all [. . .] there exists another reason which explains the absence of national music in them: it is, they have no leisure to exhale their character in songs.

William Chappell was still striving to disprove this shocking allegation several decades later. Kitchiner was probably quite correct in stating that the Celtic nations had been quicker off the mark in collecting and promoting their national song heritage.

Edinburgh's Reid Music Library, now incorporated into the main library and gradually being catalogued online, also held other items already noted as popular in St Andrews, such as Nathan's *Hebrew Melodies* and Bunting's *Ancient Music of Ireland*, not to mention other titles which may or may not have been acquired under legal deposit, such as R. A. Smith's *Scotish Minstrel*. They also kept later, post-legal deposit collections including the epic and long-lived *Songs of Scotland* edited by George Farquhar Graham and published by John Muir Wood. Indeed, one particular shelfmark seems to have been entirely

---

11 Thomas Moore, *A Selection of Popular National Airs, with Symphonies and Accomps* (London: J. Power, 1818).

12 Charles Arnim, et al., *A Selection of German National Melodies, with the Words Both in the Original and Translated into English* (London: Goulding, D'Almaine, Potter, & Co., 1816); *The Russian Troubadour; or, A Collection of Ukranian and Other National Melodies, together with the Words of Each Respective Air Translated into English Verse* (London: printed for the translator; & sold by Clementi, Banger, Collard, Davis, & Collard, 1816). Both these books are also held at the University of St Andrews.

dedicated to national melodies of various kinds, both vocal and instrumental, demonstrating a concern to collect this particular repertoire and keep it together.

It is fair to say that the surviving Georgian legal deposit music collections, viewed nationally, are something of a patchwork. In one sense, these collections came together almost as an accident of fate – libraries were entitled to the music, and some curated the music more assiduously than others. Because of the apparently haphazard way in which music was or was not registered at Stationers' Hall, even the most complete legal deposit collections do not represent everything that was published in any particular year. This circumstance has led in some libraries to an apparently random assortment of music, high-brow and low-brow, vocal and instrumental, in all the popular performing idioms of the day. This paper has focused on national song collections, but it would have been equally possible to have considered many other categories of music, such as theatrical songs or commemorative anthems.

Nevertheless, irrespective of survival patterns, the true worth of these early national tune collections is threefold. In the first instance, because they have been preserved, we can trace the historical development of whatever kind of music most interests us. Secondly, the legal deposit system as it existed in Georgian times means that in many cases there are several surviving copies around the country, facilitating study by today's scholars, wherever they may be based. Lastly, these books have immeasurable value in helping us to get inside the minds of those original compilers and collectors, professors and librarians, and to understand what they considered important. For all these reasons, we owe a debt of gratitude to the original instigators of the concept of legal deposit, who can have had little idea of the scale of what they had initiated.

'Song of the Slaughter': The Poetry and Music of Peterloo

ALISON MORGAN

In the months following the Peterloo massacre in August 1819 a panoply of poems and songs were published in the radical press and as broadside ballads. Turning to poetry and song as a vehicle for political protest was nothing new in 1819; the radical heyday of the 1790s was a time when the marriage of song and polemic was used by radicals as a primary form of expression. What is of note regarding the literature of Peterloo is the speed with which it was written and published, as well as the variety of genres employed by the largely unknown balladeers to convey the grief, rage, and horror felt by the majority of the English people at the murder and maiming of their compatriots.

This essay explores a few of these songs of Peterloo, focusing on the relationship between the newly written words and well-known tunes, whereby the meaning of both is enhanced and subverted. Another consideration is the dialogue between these songs and others written to the same tunes. Knowledge of the tune promotes the accessibility of the song, as well as increasing its memorability and facilitating the collectivity of shared singing.

In particular, this essay examines the politicization of music by the Peterloo balladeers. By writing revolutionary words to familiar songs, radicals were not only subverting the status quo but also creating unity through a communal activity. I have selected two tunes famed for their evocation of national identity, 'Rule, Britannia' and 'Scots Wha Hae' wi' Wallace Bled', to illustrate how radicals and even loyalists used them both to advocate and to contextualize the need for reform in 'the most repressive regime in modern British history'.[1]

Peterloo

On 16 August 1819, during the summer wakes holiday season, 'half of Manchester', around 60,000 men, women, and children, gathered at St Peter's Field, described by Joyce Marlow as 'the traditional home of

---

[1] Robert Reid, *The Peterloo Massacre* (London: Heinemann, 1989), p. 26.

Lancashire grievances'.[2] They marched from many outlying districts of Manchester, wearing their best clothes, carrying banners, and singing songs, including such patriotic staples as 'Rule, Britannia' and 'God Save the King'.[3] They came from Oldham and Bury, Stockport and Rochdale, to hear the famous Henry 'Orator' Hunt speak on the need for electoral reform: universal male suffrage, annual elections, and a secret ballot. It was to become one of the most significant events in modern British history.

Hunt took to the hustings at two o'clock; twenty minutes later eighteen were dead, including four women and a two-year-old child, and more than six hundred wounded by the sabres and horses' hooves of the Manchester and Salford Yeomanry Cavalry (MYC) and the Fifteenth Hussars. More than three hundred harrowing eyewitness accounts document the slaughter of that day – testimony to the brutality of the state against unarmed citizens.[4] As Robert Poole notes, 'the radicals of Lancashire planned for Victory Square, only to find themselves in Tiananmen Square'.[5] For E. P. Thompson, this was class war.[6]

News of the event spread quickly throughout the country, due in part to the publication of a lengthy article in *The Times* of 19 August by John Tyas, who was the only journalist employed by a national paper to have been present at St Peter's Field, and who was arrested along with Hunt. In the article he stresses the peaceful nature of the crowd, even when the MYC rode into their midst: 'Not a brick-bat was thrown at them – not a pistol was fired at them during this period – all was quiet and orderly.'[7] Once arrests had been made, the MYC began to attack the banners carried by the marchers, 'cutting most indiscriminately to the right and the left in order to get at them'. When the crowd began to fight back, 'From that moment the Manchester Yeomanry Cavalry lost all command of temper.'

---

[2] Joyce Marlow, *The Peterloo Massacre* (London: Rapp and Whiting, 1969), p. 60.

[3] James Epstein, *Radical Expression: Political Language, Ritual, and Symbol in England, 1790–1850* (Oxford: Oxford University Press, 1994), p. 83.

[4] Robert Poole, 'What We Don't Know about Peterloo', *Manchester Region History Review*, 23 (2014), 1–17 (pp. 3–4).

[5] Robert Poole, 'By the Law and Sword: Peterloo Revisited', *History*, 91 (2006), 254–76 (p. 276).

[6] E. P. Thompson, *The Making of the English Working Class* (Harmondsworth: Penguin, 1980 [1963]), pp. 779–80.

[7] John Tyas, 'Express from Manchester', *The Times*, 19 August 1819, p. 2.

Publication

In an ironic nod to the Battle of Waterloo fought four years previously, the journalist James Wroe, writing in the *Manchester Observer* on 21 August, named the event 'Peter Loo'.[8] Despite government and royal support for the actions of the Manchester magistrates, who had called in the yeomanry and the hussars, the reaction to the massacre was largely condemnatory and took the form not only of newspaper articles and letters but also cartoons, poetry, and even ceramics, many of which appeared within days of the massacre. Established radical periodicals, such as Thomas Wooler's *Black Dwarf*, voiced their outrage. They were briefly joined by new publications, including the *Cap of Liberty* and the *Briton*, which sprang out of the wave of protest surrounding Peterloo and then fell victim to the repressive Six Acts at the end of the year which extended stamp duty to all periodicals sold for less than sixpence, thereby silencing dissent by driving many radical publications out of existence.

Of the seventy or so Peterloo poems I have collected, almost half were published in radical periodicals, ranging from the moderate *Examiner*, with just two Peterloo poems, to the ultra-radical *Medusa* with twelve. The most prolific publisher of Peterloo verse was the *Manchester Observer*, with twenty-one poems, a few of which were later reprinted in other journals. The rest of the collection comprises broadside ballads, with a few from chapbooks. Despite many of them having 'song' in the title, only nineteen name a specific tune.[9]

Song

Poems and songs have a long-standing tradition within English vernacular culture as a swiftly produced and widely disseminated method of information, commemoration, and protest. The broadside ballad, with its diversity of subject matter and accessibility of style, was a cornerstone of vernacular culture from Tudor times until the mid-Victorian period, when the increasing circulation of newspapers led to its decline. The radical press in 1819 sought to replicate the immediacy and accessibility of the broadside as part of a wider cultural response to the events in Manchester, as well as contributing in innovative ways to the English tradition of protest poetry. The increase in literacy and greater educational opportunities at this period resulted in a democratization of culture which radical periodicals sought to exploit.

[8] *Manchester Observer*, 21 August 1819, p. 687.
[9] Alison Morgan, *Ballads and Songs of Peterloo* (Manchester: Manchester University Press, 2018).

The number of periodicals that emerged post-Waterloo indicates that there was a readership to sustain them.[10]

The use of traditional tunes for new ballads, or *contrafactum*, is commonplace throughout ballad history and is evident in a number of the Peterloo poems. Music notation was expensive to print and unintelligible to the majority of purchasers of broadsides or radical journals. However, tunes can be laden with meaning, simultaneously containing both the original words and the new. This process of defamiliarization, outlined by the Russian formalist Viktor Shklovsky, is brought about by the disruption of form, making the familiar unfamiliar, and resulting in a re-evaluation of the original content.[11] Boris Eichenbaum builds on this position, arguing that the form – in this case, the tune – is not to be regarded merely as a container into which content is poured, but as content itself.[12] I contend that the tunes explored in this essay were not selected by the Peterloo balladeers for their musical qualities but because of the meaning they contained, which would have been known to a contemporary audience.

The appropriation of the form of the broadside by radical newspapers replicates its function as 'a great meeting ground of orality and literacy'.[13] In fact, the advent of printing blurred the boundaries between oral and print culture. Steve Roud has explored the symbiotic relationship between orality and print, and notes the role played in the eighteenth century by opera, the theatres, and the pleasure gardens in disseminating songs among a wide range of social classes.[14] The broadsides, chapbooks, and songsters sold at pleasure gardens contained the songs performed there, facilitating the transfer of relatively new tunes into vernacular culture. Roud also suggests that labouring-class musicians may have played at the theatres or in the military, providing another route of transmission.[15] Eamonn O'Keefe

---

[10] Michael Scrivener (ed.), *Poetry and Reform: Periodical Verse from the English Democratic Press, 1792–1824* (Detroit: Wayne State University Press, 1992), p. 24.

[11] Victor Shklovsky, 'Art as Technique', in *Russian Formalist Criticism: Four Essays*, ed. Lee T. Lemon and Marion J. Reis (Lincoln, NE: University of Nebraska Press, 1965), p. 12.

[12] Boris Eichenbaum, 'The Formal Method', in *Readings in Russian Poetics: Formalist and Structuralist Views*, ed. Ladislav Matejka and Krystyna Pomorska (Cambridge, MA: MIT Press, 1971), p. 13.

[13] Mark W. Booth, *The Experience of Songs* (New Haven and London: Yale University Press, 1981), p. 113.

[14] Steve Roud, *Folk Song in England*, with music chapters by Julia Bishop (London: Faber & Faber, 2017), pp. 302–08.

[15] Roud, *Folk Song in England*, pp. 293–96.

has observed that many of the musicians present at Peterloo would have fought in the Napoleonic Wars, and that it was not unusual for a regimental colonel to present military musicians with their instruments when they were demobbed.[16] It could be argued that the evidence cited here explains the use of patriotic and theatrical tunes such as 'Rule, Britannia' by the Peterloo balladeers.

Anne Janowitz, too, explores the significance of the relationship between oral and print culture in the Romantic era, writing that, 'on the one hand, [it] democratis[es] print-culture poetry, and on the other, reanimate[es] the resources of oral poetic culture'.[17] Radical periodicals of the 1790s, notably Thomas Spence's *Pigs' Meat*, harnessed speed of publication to the accessibility of a familiar tune as a way of disseminating revolutionary discourse as widely as possible. Spence and his contemporary, Daniel Isaac Eaton, writer and publisher of the other great radical journal of the 1790s, *Politics for the People*, recognized the power of song to unite and disseminate political ideology. John Mee suggests that songs from *Pigs' Meat* were sung at meetings of the London Corresponding Society, of which Spence was a member, in the 1790s.[18] Michael Davis adds to this by maintaining that Spence's songs were also sung in taverns, Spence recognizing their potential to arouse and to lead to action.[19]

This tradition continued in the years following Waterloo. David Worrall cites testimony from government spies in 1817 who heard the singing of political songs at a 'free-and-easy', a tavern meeting of Spencean radicals.[20] At these gatherings political songs were 'tactically exchanged' for more innocuous ones if those assembled suspected the authorities were close by. This evidence could provide another reason for well-known tunes being used for radical songs: the tune serves in

---

[16] Lecture by Eamonn O'Keefe, 'The Musical Armed Nation: Military Musicians, Patriotism and Politics during and after the Napoleonic Wars', Music and Resistance in Europe 1815–1850, European History Research Centre, Warwick, 24 November 2018.

[17] Anne Janowitz, *Lyric and Labour in the Romantic Tradition* (Cambridge: Cambridge University Press, 1998), p. 12.

[18] John Mee, 'Thomas Spence and the London Corresponding Society, 1792–5', in *Thomas Spence: The Poor Man's Revolutionary*, ed. Alastair Bonnett and Keith Armstrong (London: Breviary Stuff Publications, 2014), pp. 53–63 (p. 58).

[19] Michael T. Davis, '"Meet and Sing, and your Chains Will Drop Off like Burnt Thread": The Political Songs of Thomas Spence', in *Thomas Spence: The Poor Man's Revolutionary*, ed. Alastair Bonnett and Keith Armstrong (London: Breviary Stuff Publications, 2014), pp. 109–25 (p. 114).

[20] David Worrall, *Radical Culture: Discourse, Resistance and Surveillance, 1790–1820* (New York and London: Harvester Wheatsheaf, 1992), pp. 92–94.

the first instance as a sort of camouflage for the words, with singers swiftly reverting to the original words, if necessary, to avoid detection. This use of and belief in the political power of song was also adopted by some publishers and balladeers in the months following Peterloo.

While it is evident that radical songs published as broadsides and in journals were sung, there is little evidence for the reception and performance of the songs written in response to Peterloo. James Epstein maintains that in Ashton-under-Lyne, on the first anniversary of the massacre, radicals paraded and sang Samuel Bamford's 'Song of the Slaughter'.[21] According to Terry Wyke, speeches, songs, and toasts were a regular feature of anniversary commemorations, although he does not state which songs were sung.[22]

Several of the songs I have collected were reprinted later in the nineteenth century. Both 'Downfall of Despotism' and 'Patriotic Song', originally published in *Medusa*, also appeared in a chapbook from 1833 entitled *Harp of Liberty*.[23] One of the most reprinted of the songs, 'Peterloo', was printed both as a broadside and in *Medusa*, where it is entitled 'The Triumph of Liberty'.[24] Many copies of the song are extant and testify to its continued popularity in the latter half of the nineteenth century. Perhaps the best known of the Peterloo songs (due, in part, to a version by The Critics Group in 1968) is the broadside *With Henry Hunt We'll Go*. Despite only a single verse and a chorus remaining of the original, John Harland and Frank Kidson published it in 1865 and 1891, respectively.[25] While there is a continuity of publication of only a few of the songs sung in the years after Peterloo, it does suggest that they were not as ephemeral as the publications in which they were first printed.

The two case studies I explore below demonstrate the different ways in which tune and words combined to present very different views of English identity. In the case of 'Rule, Britannia', we see how the text works in conjunction with and in opposition to the original song, the process of defamiliarization enabling the listener to hear the

---

[21] Epstein, *Radical Expression*, p. 156. 'Song of the Slaughter' was set to the tune 'Sicilian Mariners' Hymn', also known as 'O Sanctissima'.

[22] Terry Wyke, 'Remembering the Manchester Massacre', in *Return to Peterloo*, ed. Robert Poole (Manchester: Manchester Centre for Regional History, [2014]), pp. 111–31 (p. 113).

[23] Morgan, *Ballads and Songs of Peterloo*, p. 203.

[24] Morgan, *Ballads and Songs of Peterloo*, pp. 199–200.

[25] John Harland, *Ballads and Songs of Lancashire* (London: Whittaker, 1865), pp. 261–62; Frank Kidson (ed.), *Traditional Tunes: A Collection of Ballad Airs* (Oxford: Chas. Taphouse & Son, 1891), pp. 161–63.

song anew by comparing the different versions. 'Scots Wha Hae' is a song of protest selected by radical balladeers to align the experience of the embattled and repressed Englishman with that of the Scot.

'Rule, Britannia'

Today, 'Rule, Britannia' is associated with the flag-waving, Union Jack-swathed Last Night of the Proms with its ostentatious display of Britishness. In the Romantic period, however, the tune was appropriated by radicals as a way of questioning established notions of patriotism. Patriotism was a disputed concept: for loyalists, defined as 'love of or devotion to one's country',[26] it was displayed through unequivocal support for king, church, and state; radicals, on the other hand, employed what has been described by Janowitz as 'oppositional patriotism' to underpin their belief that a true Englishman defends his ancient rights and liberties against the foreign monarchy and Francophile aristocracy.[27]

The choice of patriotic tunes for radical songs dates back to the mid-eighteenth century when 'Rule, Britannia' and 'God Save the King' were written.[28] They were selected by radical balladeers to intensify the satire of their words, thereby subverting the imperial tenor of the original and conveying the ideals of liberty from oppression and tyranny. By taking tunes associated with the establishment, the balladeers were reclaiming British identity.

The words for 'Rule, Britannia' were written by James Thomson and set to music by the composer Thomas Arne, who was also responsible for the revival of 'God Save the King'. 'Rule, Britannia' was originally composed for David Mallet's masque *Alfred*, first performed in August 1740 for Frederick, Prince of Wales. As is common with courtly masques, this panegyric champions a jingoistic Whig patriotism, comparing the German Prince of Wales with the English King Alfred, who was regarded by many English radicals as a figurehead.[29] As with 'God Save the King', 'Rule, Britannia' achieved widespread popularity following its performance at the Drury Lane theatre in 1745 during the Jacobite rebellion, when the forces led by

---

[26] *Oxford English Dictionary*, patriotism, *n*. https://www.oed.com/.

[27] Janowitz, *Lyric and Labour in the Romantic Tradition*, p. 86.

[28] For radical versions of the national anthem, see Alison Morgan, '"God Save Our Queen!": Percy Bysshe Shelley and Radical Appropriations of the British National Anthem', *Romanticism*, 20 (2014), 60–72.

[29] Christopher Hill, *Puritanism and Revolution* (London: Pimlico, 2001 [1958]), pp. 96–97.

Charles Edward Stuart succeeded in getting as far as Derby, much to the alarm of the British state. It begins:

When Britain first, at heaven's command,
Arose from out the azure main,
This was the charter of the land,
And Guardian Angels sang this strain:
Rule, Britannia! Britannia, rule the waves!
Britons never, never, never shall be slaves.

In the 1790s the tune made several appearances in Spence's *Pigs' Meat*, including with 'A Song', written in New York by R. H. in 1793, which lambasts British imperialism for 'banish[ing] peace from Afric's shore', subverting the original proclamation that 'Britons never, never, never shall be slaves' and calling on Britannia to 'view the waves, / On which thy darling sons are slaves'.[30] Enslaved by their own colonialism, the British have forfeited liberty, claimed by many as so central to its national identity. In the original song, after defeating the 'haughty tyrants' of other nations, Britannia 'repairs' to 'thy happy coast' to 'guard the fair'. In this song, which closely parodies the original, following Britannia's failed attempts to control other nations, liberty flees from 'thy venal court', 'To sing on Gallia's fre'er ground / Or breathe Columbia's purer air'. For Spenceans, liberty was to be found in France and America rather than Britain. The grandstanding imperialism of the original song adds force to the satirical tone of the parody, clearly illustrating how patriotism was a contested idea in the Romantic period.

While Spence and like-minded radicals were appropriating the tune of 'Rule, Britannia' to shed light on the enslavement both of Britons and of colonized peoples, loyalists chose the tune to showcase their own form of patriotism during the French Revolutionary Wars. The aptly titled 'Church and King' was published in the conservative *Gentleman's Magazine* in March 1793.[31] The song laments the 'bleeding corpse of France', which was 'by too much Liberty undone', and calls upon sympathizers to 'go, democratic demons, go!'. Mourning the enslavement of the king and the flight of the nobility, the anonymous balladeer exhorts the listener, 'Let Britons then united sing, / Old England's glory, – church and king.'

---

[30] *Pigs' Meat*, 3 vols (London, 1793–95), II, 67.
[31] Betty T. Bennett (ed.), *British War Poetry in the Age of Romanticism, 1793–1815* (New York: Garland, 1976), pp. 71–73.

The appeal to 'Old England' appeared in both radical and loyalist discourse. For loyalists it represented the domination of the monarch with the support of the established church, whereas for radicals it evoked the ancient rights and democratic values of the Anglo-Saxons, which had been threatened and eroded by every monarch since William the Conqueror. This myth of the 'Norman yoke' is of great historical significance and has probably persisted in oral tradition since 1066.[32] It appears, for example, in 'The Watch Word of Britons', one of the Peterloo songs written to the tune of 'Rule, Britannia', published in the ultra-radical weekly periodical *Medusa* on 25 September 1819.[33] The call to reclaim lost rights and throw off the 'abject yoke' is a common trope within radical discourse. Harking back to the past is regarded as less threatening than a desire to change the status quo: restitution rather than revolution. However, the 'watch word' of the song, 'give us death or liberty', echoes the journal's distinctly revolutionary motto: 'Let's die like men, and not be sold likes slaves' – a quotation from John Philip Kemble's 1795 play *Venice Preserv'd*, an unlikely inspiration for an ultra-radical journal.

Published by Thomas Davison in Smithfield, *Medusa; or, Penny Politician* ran for forty-six issues from February 1819 until January 1820 and cost one penny, making it affordable to the labouring classes and demonstrating that Peterloo was of interest beyond the north-west. The journal's tone, described as one of 'determined insolence',[34] is evident in the dozen or so poems it published on Peterloo:

Arouse! arouse! ye freemen brave,
And claim the rights your fathers held:
Prepare, prepare, these rights to save
Tyrants basely have withheld.

Chorus:
This is our Watch word – our watch word this shall be –
'Or give us death or liberty.'

Too long beneath an abject yoke
We basely bowed nor dar'd complain;
The magic charm – the spell is broke
And tyrants shall no longer reign.

---

[32] Hill, *Puritanism and Revolution*, pp. 53–56.
[33] Morgan, *Ballads and Songs of Peterloo*, pp. 53–55.
[34] Paul Keen (ed.), *The Popular Radical Press in Britain, 1817–21*, 6 vols (London: Pickering and Chatto, 2003), V, 1.

Can monarchs quench their rising flame
Which grows in ev'ry patriot's breast?
Shall freedom still be but a name,
Untamely we be still oppressed?

Are bloodhounds in the shape of men
Allow'd to slay a harmless race?
Shall they imbrue their hands again,
And we permit the foul disgrace?

Oh Freedom! be thou still our guide,
Still ev'ry heart be fixed on thee;
For gods behold with joy and pride,
A nation struggling to be free!

The man who nobly joins thy band,
And fearless dare thy foes engage,
Immortalized his name shall stand
Enroll'd in hist'ry's brightest page!

Textually, this song is entirely different from the original 'Rule, Britannia', but it can be assumed that readers of *Medusa* would have been familiar with the tune. Even though 'Rule, Britannia' was composed for an aristocratic masque, numerous versions of the song appeared as broadsides and in songsters. This was not uncommon, and other tunes such as Handel's 'See the Conquering Hero Comes' and Garrick's 'Heart of Oak' were likewise employed by the Peterloo balladeers, the transgression of class boundaries another example of the reclamation of British identity.

In calling on 'freemen' to 'arouse' in the opening line of the song, 'The Watch Word of Britons' can be described as an exhortatory ballad or 'apostrophe', a number of which were published after Peterloo. It would appear that these calls-to-arms escaped the notice of the authorities – who, one supposes, would have regarded them as evidence of sedition.[35] This rallying cry also chimes with a definition for 'watchword' used in the eighteenth and nineteenth centuries as 'A preconcerted signal to begin an attack'.[36] The 'Britannia' of the original song is no longer a figurehead for imperial ambition but a

---

[35] Mary Thrale (ed.), *Selections from the Papers of the London Corresponding Society, 1792–99* (Cambridge: Cambridge University Press: 1983), p. 168, cites court transcripts of the accused being questioned about radical songs.
[36] *Oxford English Dictionary*, watchword, *n.*, 2.a. https://www.oed.com/.

symbol of the common man, anxious to reclaim both land and rights long ago surrendered to 'tyrants'.

'Scots Wha Hae wi' Wallace Bled'

Along with 'God Save the King', it is unsurprising that 'Rule, Britannia' became a symbol of the claim and counterclaim on English and British identity during the turbulent period of the 1790s–1810s. The second tune I wish to focus on, 'Scots Wha Hae wi' Wallace Bled', has altogether different connotations, although its patriotic links are still as strong. It remains the anthem of the Scottish Nationalist Party and is sung each year at the close of the party conference.

Robert Burns used a traditional Scottish tune, 'Hey Tuttie Tatie' (supposedly an imitation of the sound of either a trumpet or a drum), for his song 'Bruce's Address to his Troops at the Battle of Bannockburn', the first line of which gave rise to the more commonly known title. It is widely believed that 'Hey Tuttie Tatie' was played by the army of Robert the Bruce at the Battle of Bannockburn in 1314, and it is also the tune (as so many are, including 'God Save the King') for a Jacobite drinking song, entitled 'Fill Up Your Bumpers High'. Published anonymously in the *Morning Chronicle* in 1794, Murray Pittock claims: 'Burns' song can be interpreted as a criticism of the contemporaneous oppressors of the Scots – the Hanoverians – as well as the historical oppression of the Plantagenets.'[37] The song begins:

> Scots, wha hae wi' Wallace bled,
> Scots, wham Bruce has aften led,
> Welcome to your gory bed, –
> Or to victorie.

Bruce prepares his men for battle, calling on their courage and patriotism:

> Lay the proud Usurpers low!
> Tyrants fall in every foe!
> Liberty's in every blow!
> Let us do or die!!!

The combination of Jacobite and Jacobin sentiment within the song would have appealed to a contemporary audience. Although Burns's

---

[37] Murray Pittock, *Poetry and Jacobite Politics in Eighteenth-Century Britain and Ireland* (Cambridge: Cambridge University Press, 1994), pp. 218–19.

song is about Bruce, Wallace features in numerous radical songs as a revered example of a warrior who took on the might of the colonial oppressor to defend his nation. It is easy to see how, like the Norman yoke cited above, such a symbol would appeal to radical English nationalists.

Three Peterloo poems are written to 'Scots Wha Hae wi' Wallace Bled', demonstrating the significance of the rebel patriot at a time when the radical movement was in dire need of strong leadership. According to John Tyas's eyewitness report in *The Times*, one of the banners at Peterloo was inscribed with the motto of Sir William Wallace, 'God armeth the Patriot', an indication that Wallace was a widely known figure at the time. 'The Manchester Massacre; or, Adieu to Slavery' was published around 1820 in *The Radical Reformers New Song Book*, a chapbook published by John Marshall, Newcastle radical and printer.[38] Little is known about Marshall, but it means that news of, and interest in, Peterloo extended to the north-east:

England, roused as from a sleep,
Finds abundant cause to weep,
Sees her Sons in blood lie deep,
With horror and dismay.

Her Daughters too, do not go free,
But in the common blood-shed see,
Children share the same mercy,
From the Cavalry.

Can Britons see this awful sight,
And not cry out, We'll boldly fight,
So long as blood doth give us might,
To gain our Liberty.

See yon Scots! How dear the name,
Who with Wallace nobly came,
To fight for Freedom was their aim;
Behold your Pattern.

Britons' rights you must maintain,
Let freedom be your only aim,
Now throw off your heavy chain;
Adieu to Slavery.

---

[38] Morgan, *Ballads and Songs of Peterloo*, pp. 56–57.

To see Sir Francis, or the Star,
To join your force he will prefer,
Then let your actions now declare
You worthy of your head.

The balladeer presents the listener with the 'awful sight' of Britain's sons and daughters lying deep in blood, and uses both tune and words to draw comparisons with Wallace in the fourth stanza, before calling on Britons to 'throw off your heavy chain' – an unconscious allusion to Shelley's famous proclamation in *The Masque of Anarchy*, 'Shake your chains to earth like dew.' The utilization of a Scottish symbol of freedom to promote an English cause demonstrates a conscious aim to link Jacobite and Jacobin. Manchester showed considerable support for the Jacobites in the eighteenth century, and the figure of Wallace suggests that radical Lancastrians felt more affinity with their Scottish neighbours than with the English elite.[39]

'Song' was published in the *Manchester Observer* on 9 October 1819.[40] As mentioned above, the *Manchester Observer* published the greatest number of Peterloo poems and songs. Established in January 1818, by the end of 1819 its circulation was close to 12,000 per week, although a number of libel cases exacerbated the precariousness of its finances and led to its demise in 1821.[41] Its editors, John Saxton, James Wroe, and John Knight, were founding members of the Patriotic Union Society which invited Henry Hunt to speak in August 1819. Knight and Saxton were arrested alongside Hunt and sent to the New Bailey Prison in Salford. 'Song' makes no reference to Wallace, but draws instead upon English republican heroes:

Whigs! Whose ancestors were wont
Of fruitless power to stand the brunt,
Nor leave, like you, to shoot, or hunt,
Sweet Freedom's cause.

Cause, by the virtuous HAMPDEN led –
Cause, for which SYDNEY, RUSSELL, bled,
When e'en o'er you its glory shed –
Oh, turn and pause!

Peers! Gentlemen! Can ye lie by
When *vultures* hover in the sky?

---

[39] Stuart Hylton, *A History of Manchester* (Andover: Phillimore, 2010), p. 39.
[40] Morgan, *Ballads and Songs of Peterloo*, pp. 75–77.
[41] Thompson, *Making of the English Working Class*, p. 742.

When, *without Inquest*, Freemen die?
Untimely fall.

Can ye make *game* your only care,
Nor, from your toil one moment spare,
To question *other massacre*!
Rouse, one and all!

Cause, by the virtuous HAMPDEN led –
Cause for which SYDNEY, RUSSELL bled,
When e'en o'er you its glory shed –
Oh, turn and pause!

As with many radical songs of the Romantic period, the author invokes seventeenth-century opponents of despotic rule, harnessing their cause to that of the nineteenth-century radicals. Widely regarded as Republican martyrs, John Hampden, Algernon Sydney, and William Russell opposed the Catholic tendencies of the monarch and his heir. Both Sydney and Russell were executed for treason in 1683 following their failed ambush of Charles II and his brother, James. Hampden was pardoned. With the allusion to Wallace embodied in the tune, these balladeers were encouraging their audiences to locate themselves within a continuum of radical patriots who actively opposed the state in order to reinstate the true national identity and to challenge tyrannical rule. As with so many of the Peterloo songs, it leads up to a call-to-arms: 'Rouse, one and all!'

The third Peterloo song written to the tune of 'Scots Wha Hae', 'Britons Who Have Often Bled', published in the *Republican* on 15 October 1819, also invokes the figure of Hampden in its opening stanza.[42] The *Republican* was published by Richard Carlile, who was present at Peterloo and was due to appear on the hustings along with Henry Hunt. Unlike Hunt and many others, Carlile was not arrested and he printed his eyewitness account of the massacre five days later, on 21 August, in *Sherwin's Political Register*, which was rebranded as the *Republican* in early September. It is not known whether Carlile himself wrote 'Britains Who Have Often Bled', although the style mirrors that of his prose writings in the *Republican*, including his article about Peterloo under the headline 'Horrid Massacre at Manchester'.[43] Despite Carlile's notoriety for having published pirate copies of

---

[42] Morgan, *Ballads and Songs of Peterloo*, pp. 71–72.
[43] *Sherwin's Weekly Political Register*, 10.5 (1819), 237.

Shelley's revolutionary poem *Queen Mab*, little poetry appeared in the *Republican*, which published only two Peterloo poems.

Although the tune is not named in the *Republican*, the form of the song, together with the textual similarity to the original, makes it clear to the reader that it was intended to be sung to 'Scots Wha Hae':

Britons who have often bled
In the cause that Hampden led,
Welcome to your gory bed,
    Or to Victory.

Now's the day, and now's the hour,
See the front of battle lour,
See approach your Tyrant's power,
    Chains and slavery.

Who would be a traitor knave?
Who would fill a coward's grave?
Who so base as to be a slave?
    Traitor, coward, turn and flee!

Who at Liberty's sweet cry
Freedom's sword would raise on high?
Freeman stand, or freeman die,
    Hark! Your chief cries, 'On with me!'

By Oppression's woes and pains,
By your sons in servile chains,
We will drain our dearest veins,
    But they shall be free!

Lay your proud oppressors low!
Tyrants fall in every blow!
For the cause of God below,
    In the cause of Liberty.

When this version is compared with Burns's original it is evident that very few words have been changed. The 'Scots' have been replaced by 'Britons', with 'Hampden' as opposed to 'Bruce' as their leader. While Burns names Edward II as the oppressor, here it is an unnamed 'Tyrant', suggesting that the balladeer either thought it judicious not to name the king, or meant that all monarchs were tyrants. As with the original, the people are presented with a choice between revolution, slavery, or death, and are exhorted to fight, not for Scotland, but for Liberty.

* * *

These few songs about Peterloo highlight the way in which balladeers drew on traditions of vernacular and radical culture by setting new words to tunes laden with meaning. Naming a well-known tune would, I contest, have helped ensure that these songs that were more widely disseminated by promoting their accessibility and collective performance. With familiar tunes and easily remembered refrains, their revolutionary sentiment would have been heard in the taverns and meeting houses of London and beyond – as part of what Janowitz calls the 'communitarian lyric', whereby the ballad was central to the plebeian culture of the time through its combination of the political, the poetic, and the communal.[44]

The links across the centuries, whether established implicitly via the tune or explicitly through the naming of past heroes, place these songs within the tradition of protest song. Those seeking to express and disseminate their outrage at events in Manchester on 16 August 1819 followed in a centuries-old tradition. By choosing the medium of song as a vehicle for the anger, grief, and desire for retribution felt by a downtrodden people after the Peterloo massacre, these unknown balladeers captured this seminal event in British history and were able to communicate it across two hundred years to a modern audience. In an era in which democracy is under siege and xenophobic nationalism on the rise, these songs are highly relevant. It is rewarding to know that with the bicentenary of Peterloo, and in years to come, these songs will once again be heard on the streets of Manchester and beyond.[45]

---

[44] Janowitz, *Lyric and Labour in the Romantic Tradition*, p. 8.
[45] https://theroadtopeterloo.com/.

From Siege to Songbook: Late Medieval Folk Song as Political Memory

LINDE NUYTS

Over the past decades, literary scholars and cultural historians have demonstrated that literary production is strongly intertwined with the representation of the self and with the collective memories of social groups.[1] This approach is particularly promising for the genre of 'historical' or 'political' songs – that is, vernacular songs dealing with past and contemporary historical events. Political folk songs, more than other genres dealing with politics, can give us information about common experiences of politics and popular opinions. However, the corpus of political songs in the late medieval Low Countries, although well inventoried, has not yet received the attention it deserves.[2]

In this paper I focus on a song that tells the story of the 1489 siege of the Flemish coastal town of Nieuwpoort, the second largest port city of Flanders. It is preserved in just one copy, in the *Antwerp Songbook* of 1544. The fifty-five years and 130 kilometres between siege and songbook demonstrate the considerable impact the song

* I would like to thank Jan Dumolyn, Veerle Fraeters, Frank Willaert, Samuel Mareel, Jelle Haemers, David Murray, and Brianne Dolce for their help and comments.

[1] Erika Kuijpers, Judith Pollmann, and J. Steen, *Memory before Modernity* (Leiden: Brill, 2016); Jan Assmann, *Cultural Memory and Early Civilization: Writing, Remembrance, and Political Imagination* (Cambridge: Cambridge University Press, 2011); Wendy Scase, *Literature and Complaint in England, 1272–1553* (Oxford: Oxford University Press, 2007); Tom Cheesman, *The Shocking Ballad Picture Show: German Popular Literature and Cultural History* (Oxford: Berg, 1994); Jan Bloemendal, Arjan van Dixhoorn, and Elsa Strietman, *Literary Cultures and Public Opinion in the Low Countries, 1450–1650* (Leiden: Brill, 2011).

[2] For the Low Countries, the possibilities for such research were pointed out by Jan Dumolyn and Jelle Haemers, 'Political Poems and Subversive Songs: The Circulation of "Public Poetry" in the Late Medieval Low Countries', *Journal of Dutch Literature*, 5 (2014), 1–22. See also Éva Guillorel, 'Folksongs, Conflicts and Social Protest in Early Modern France', in *Identity, Intertextuality, and Performance in Early Modern Song Culture*, ed. Dieuwke van der Poel, Louis Peter Grijp, and Wim van Anrooij (Leiden: Brill, 2016), pp. 287–307; Volker Honemann, 'Politische Lieder und Sprüche im späten Mittelalter und der frühen Neuzeit', *Die Musikforschung*, 50 (1997), 399–421; Rosa Salzberg and Massimo Rospocher, 'Street Singers in Italian Renaissance Urban Culture and Communication', *Cultural and Social History*, 9 (2012), 9–26; Una McIlvenna, 'When the News Was Sung: Ballads as News Media in Early Modern Europe', *Media History*, 22 (2016), 317–33.

must have had, making it a useful case study to understand the function and impact of a political song. My analysis will show how a political event was lived and remembered by the less literate groups of late medieval society, those that are often omitted from historical narratives.

The 1489 siege of Nieuwpoort took place in the context of a series of Flemish revolts against Maximilian of Habsburg between 1482 and 1492. An alliance of nobles and townspeople from Bruges, Ghent, and Ypres revolted against the loss of autonomy imposed by the Habsburg prince.[3] In 1489, the rebels tried to conquer the Flemish coast with the help of French royal troops. They hoped for an easy victory in Nieuwpoort, a port town which was suffering heavy economic losses due to the conflict. Nieuwpoort proved stronger than expected and withstood the siege. An annual procession was organized to commemorate these events, cementing the place of this tough victory in the collective urban memory. All citizens of Nieuwpoort, dressed up and organized in groups according to their roles in the town, walked along the walls carrying a statue of the Virgin of Mercy who had protected the city during the siege. The celebration included a market, a theatre competition, and, of course, dancing and drinking. In addition to the yearly festivities, the citizens kept a candle burning for the Virgin Mary, admired the stained-glass window installed in recognition of their loyalty during the siege, and named a tower after the enemy.[4] Such a strong culture of urban memory must have been a perfect breeding ground for this triumphant song.[5]

What was the place of this song within the culture of urban memory? What was the reception and function of the song beyond its local context? Was it sung only because of its catchy melody, or did it have political significance in its new context(s)? To understand the impact and function of the song, it is crucial to know more about its origin and circulation. How was it created and for what occasion? Who performed it, where, when, and why? For what audiences was it

---

[3] Jelle Haemers, *De strijd om het regentschap over Filips de Schone: Opstand, facties en geweld in Brugge, Gent en Ieper (1482–1488)* (Ghent: Academia Press, 2014); Jelle Haemers, 'Factionalism and State Power in the Flemish Revolt (1482–1492)', *Journal of Social History*, 42 (2009), 1009–39.

[4] Edward Vlietinck, *1489–1889: Eene bladzijde uit de geschiedenis der stad Nieupoort* (Oostende: Vlietinck, 1889), pp. 98–121; Joannes Baptista Rybens, *Beschryving der stad ende haven van Nieuport in het graefschap Vlaenderen* (Nieuwpoort: Heemkring Bachten De Kupe, 1966), pp. 7–12.

[5] Judith Pollmann, *Memory in Early Modern Europe, 1500–1800* (Oxford: Oxford University Press, 2017), pp. 93–118, discusses the siege of Leiden in 1574 which led to a very similar culture of urban memory.

sung? Was it transmitted in writing or orally? Such questions of context are a challenge when using songs as sources for cultural history. Folk songs are interesting sources because of their 'popular' nature – popular in the sense that the genre is open to everyone, especially to the non-elite, people with limited access to education, means, and power.[6] As with most folk songs, the author of this song is not known. No other sources refer to the performance of the song.

Nevertheless, it is possible to gather information about the functions and impact of the song. First, there is information about the collection within which the Nieuwpoort song is found, the *Antwerp Songbook*. Its presence in this collection provides some information about what type of song it was, why it was sung, and on what occasions. Secondly, the words of the song provide hints as to its origin and transmission. Thirdly, several *contrafacta* (songs composed to an existing melody) of the Nieuwpoort song have been identified, the oldest dating from Nieuwpoort in 1511, showing that it originated before that date, probably locally, and providing further clues as to its context of circulation. Songbook, words, and *contrafacta* will together help elucidate the song's functions and impact on its road from siege to songbook and beyond.

The *Antwerp Songbook*

The *Antwerp Songbook* is the oldest preserved printed secular song collection of the Low Countries. The one surviving complete version of the booklet was printed in 1544 in Antwerp, which was at that time one of the most important centres of the printing industry in Europe. It was priced at around one tenth of a daily craftsman's wage and therefore must have been affordable for a large audience; it does not include music notation, but the songs were well known and are arranged alphabetically, 'so that you would easily find the song you wish to sing'. This sentence in the introduction stresses the popularity of the chosen songs; one would use the book to look up the words of a song one already knew.[7]

The printer tried to reach out to all corners of sixteenth-century society. The songs contained something for everyone's interest – love, sex, city life, and so on. They are titled either 'new' or 'old', probably to alert the audience to the songs appropriate to their generation. The 'old songs' go back an average of fifty years before the songbook,

---

6 Peter Burke, *Popular Culture in Early Modern Europe* (London: Temple Smith, 1978).
7 Dieuwke van der Poel, et al., *Het Antwerps Liedboek* (Tielt: Lannoo, 2004), pp. 9–45.

around the time of the siege of Nieuwpoort.[8] Based on the price and themes, a broad, popular audience can be inferred for the songbook. We have to keep in mind that commercial motives might have had an influence on the contents of the songs; the compiler might have left out parts that seemed less appealing, or else have shortened songs that took up too much space.

When looking for the possible audience for a particular song in a printed songbook, one would assume literacy to be a criterion, in addition to price, practicality, and subject matter. However, a written or printed song was not only sung by the literate. The songs in commercial books of this kind were no more than a selection from the wide range of orally circulating songs, selected for the book-buying elite. Even illiterate people could buy a broadsheet of a song they particularly liked and if they forgot the words they could go to a literate neighbour with their broadsheet and fill in the gaps in their memory.[9]

The compiler of the songbook clearly wanted to reduce all obstacles to his intended audience buying the book. However, he was not free from obstacles himself when choosing songs, but had to navigate around possible political censorship.[10] Thus self-censorship might have influenced the choice of songs. This is illustrated by the later prohibition of the songbook, and there is some evidence of (self-)censorship, mainly of satires directed at the clergy, in surviving fragments of later versions of the songbook. In sum, the song in question is part of a collection of songs that were chosen, and maybe even altered, for profit. We need to bear in mind that there were probably other versions – written or oral – of the song in circulation.

Text, origin, circulation

What about the social environments in which the song circulated during the thirty-three years separating the printing of the songbook

---

[8] C. Vellekoop, 'Hoe Oud Is "Oudt" in Het Antwerps Liedboek?', in *Tussentijds: Bundel studies aangeboden aan W. P. Gerritsen ter gelegenheid van zijn vijftigste verjaardag*, ed. A. M. J. van Buuren, et al. (Utrecht: HES, 1985), pp. 272–79.

[9] Pollmann, *Memory in Early Modern Europe*, pp. 95–96. Katell Lavéant, 'Drama and Urban Literacy: Recording and Documenting the Performance in the Southern Low Countries (Fifteenth-Sixteenth Centuries)', in *Medieval Urban Literacy, II: Uses of the Written Word in Medieval Towns*, ed. Marco Mostert and Anna Adamska (Turnhout: Brepols, 2014), pp. 375–87; René Ernst Victor Stuip and Cornelis Vellekoop, *Oraliteit en Schriftcultuur* (Hilversum: Verloren, 1993); Bloemendal, van Dixhoorn, and Strietman, *Literary Cultures and Public Opinion in the Low Countries*.

[10] van der Poel, et al., *Het Antwerps Liedboek*, pp. 31–33.

from the oldest trace of the song, the *contrafactum* dating from 1511? Here, features of the text itself, as well as some of its formal characteristics, may provide some clues. Textual traces can only be relevant for analysis when the song is understood in context.[11] One group of 'intertexts' is the *Antwerp Songbook* itself, containing 224 songs of similar length, all fashionable around 1544 and printed from commercial motives. Another group consists of narratives on the same topic, the siege of Nieuwpoort in 1489.

Even though the *Antwerp Songbook* constitutes a 'unity', printed for a single audience, there are songs of different types within the book, with similarities in narrative structure, formal complexity, theme, and language. Identifying these song types within the songbook would facilitate the inference of performance contexts in which certain song types and styles would have been appropriate. The ways in which this individual song differs from songs of the same type would then highlight its peculiarities, leading to a better understanding of its specific origins and circulation.[12]

However, these popular songs have not been substantively grouped into song types. W. P. Gerritsen provided a starting point for a classification of the songs in the *Antwerp Songbook* based on structural characteristics. He maintained that when the songs are ordered structurally, they display similarities that extent beyond each grouping.[13] I start from Gerritsen's classification to understand how the narrative structure of this song might provide information about

---

[11] On the links between language and social history, see Peter Burke, *Towards a Social History of Early Modern Dutch* (Amsterdam: Amsterdam University Press, 2010); Peter Burke, Roy Porter, and Ruth Finnegan, *The Social History of Language* (Cambridge: Cambridge University Press, 1987). For scholars who connect late medieval literary characteristics with cultural tendencies, see *inter alia* Wendy Scase, 'Imagining Alternatives to the Book: The Transmission of Political Poetry in Late Medieval England', in *Imagining the Book*, ed. Stephen Kelly and John J. Thompson (Turnhout: Brepols, 2005), pp. 237–50; Paul Strohm, *Hochon's Arrow: The Social Imagination of Fourteenth-Century Texts* (Princeton: Princeton University Press, 2014); Cheesman, *Shocking Ballad Picture Show*.

[12] Joris Reynaert, 'Onhoofse liederen: Thematische genres en types in het gruuthuseliedboek.', in *Een zoet akkoord: Middeleeuwse lyriek in de Lage Landen*, ed. Frank Willaert (Amsterdam: Prometheus, 1992), pp. 154–69, writes about 'genre-dependency' and how in Dutch this has only been studied for love songs.

[13] W. P. Gerritsen, 'Het Antwerps Liedboek', in *Het Antwerps Liedboek, 87 melodieën op teksten uit 'Een Schoon Liedekens-Boeck' van 1544* (Amsterdam: Vereniging voor Nederlandse Muziekgeschiedenis, 1972), pp. viii–xli. See also van der Poel, et al., *Het Antwerps Liedboek*, pp. 11–24.

its performance.[14] Almost half the songs from the *Antwerp Songbook* were classified by Gerritsen as a type in which the story is told by an external narrator who does not intervene in the story. These songs often start or end with a poetic formula in which the narrator manifests himself in the role of the singer.[15] Our song, too, ends with such a 'poet stanza', which suggests oral, public performance.[16] Songs of this type also have a loose structure, with confusing dialogue, which can be taken as a sign of orality and age.

The songs in the *Antwerp Songbook* have a variety of rhyme schemes. Some are complicated or follow fixed forms such as ballads, pointing towards a specialized, cultured writer or performer. Others, like this one, have uncomplicated rhyme schemes. The rhyme scheme is *aba'bcdc* – only for two stressed lines (*b* and *c*) do the final words need to rhyme. This simple rhyme scheme points away from singers who composed songs for artistic purposes, or 'rhetoricians'.[17] In contrast, it suggests looser, more popular performance situations, such as in the street or tavern. Yet even though the rhyme scheme is simple, it is not uniform. First, the *a'* lines vary in rhyme and accent. Also, the length and number of accents in each stanza are different. The fourth stanza lacks a stressed *c* rhyme. The final stanza has a rhyme scheme of *ababbcb*. This more rigid scheme is harder to follow and suggests that this final 'poet stanza' was either changed or added later on. The 'poet stanza' is also more amenable to change because it is not part of the narrative.

The lack of uniformity suggests oral transmission.[18] Inter-strophic

---

[14] The translation opposite is my 'Middle English' rendering of the song text, which attempts to maintain the spirit of the Middle Dutch original. I would like to thank Julie van Bogaert, Zia Foley, and Frank Willaert for their help.

[15] Gerritsen, 'Het Antwerps Liedboek', pp. xxii–xxvii.

[16] There is no research yet explicitly connecting 'poet stanzas' with their performance context but the postscript to the latest edition of the *Antwerp Songbook* appears to refer to this in relation to 'songs written in the oral style' (van der Poel, et al., *Het Antwerps Liedboek*, pp. 14–18).

[17] Characteristic of later medieval literary culture in the Low Countries were poets and playwrights, mostly from the upper middle classes of guild-masters and merchants, organized in urban literary guilds or confraternities. See Anne-Laure Van Bruaene, *Om beters wille: Rederijkerskamers en de stedelijke cultuur in de Zuidelijke Nederlanden (1400–1650)* (Amsterdam: Amsterdam University Press, 2010); Anne-Laure van Bruaene, 'The Chambers of Rhetoric in the (Southern) Low Countries: A Flemish-Dutch Project on Literary Confraternities', *Confraternitas*, 16 (2005), 3–14.

[18] W. P. Gerritsen, 'Jan en Jenneken en de mondelinge overlevering van balladen', in *Een zoet akkoord: Middeleeuwse lyriek in de Lage Landen*, ed. Frank Willaert (Amsterdam: Prometheus, 1992), pp. 287–302; van der Poel, et al., *Het Antwerps Liedboek*, pp. 14–18.

'Een oudt liedeken'	'An old song'
Souuereyn van Vlaenderen	Sovereign-bailiff of Flanders
Laet sincken uwen moet	Let thy courage sink
Wilt v gheuanghen gheuen	Give thyself as captive
Behouden lijf ende goet	Save thy life and possessions
Voor Nyeupoort willen wi maken spel	For Nieuwpoort we want to fight
Nv swijghet verrader stille	Now be quiet, traitor
V meninghe verstae ic wel	Thy intention I understand
Soude ic mi gheuanghen gheuen	Shall I give myself as captive
Ic en ben noch niet veruaert	I am not afraid
Ic rijde hier lancx die mueren	I ride here along the walls
Ick sitte hie op mijn paert	I sit here on my horse
Ic gheue den ruyters goden moet	I give the soldiers divine courage
Ick drincke den wijn wt schalen	I drink wine from beakers
Ghelijck menich stout ruyter doet	Like many an audacious rider doth
Herman die op der clocken sloech	Herman rang the bell
Hi sach int Fransche heyr	He saw in the French army
Wel op ghi borgers van Nieupoort	Stand up ye burghers of Nieuwpoort
Stelt v nv vromelick ter weyr	Withstand valiantly
Want ons en gaet geen slapen aen	Because we are not entitled to sleep
Ick sie die Fransche knechten	I see the French soldiers
Blanck in haer harnas staen	White in their armour
Si quamen daer aengedrongen	They advanced there
Veel blancker dan een ijs	Much whiter than ice
Op eenen morgenstonde	At daybreak
Si behaelden daer cleynen prijs	They won there a scanty prize
Creuecoor met alle zijnder macht	Crèvecoeur with all his force
Nyeupoort hout v vast	Nieuwpoort stand fast
Ghi en sult niet ghewonnen zijn	Thou shalt not be defeated
Die Zwitsers met haren cransen	Those Swiss with their hats
si lagen daer al versmoort	They lay there all smothered
Si en hadden gheen herte om dansen	They had no heart for dancing
Dies truerde creuecoor	Thus deplored Crèvecoeur
Dat hi was comen sonder auijs	That he had come without good counsel
Al voor dat stedeken van Nyeu poort	Before that city of Nieuwpoort
Hi behaelde daer cleynen prijs	He won there a scanty prize
Die dit liedeken dichte	Who rhymeth this song
Dat was een ruyter goet	It was a rider good
Hi faelgeerde in zijn gesichte	He had bad eyesight
Dies truerde hi in sinen moet	That's why his heart was sad
hy bidt maria die maghet soet	He prays to Mary the Virgin sweet
Dat si dat soete Vlaenderlant	That she take that sweet land of Flanders
Wilt nemen in haer behoet.	Under her protection.

(van der Poel, et al., *Het Antwerps Liedboek*, p. 328.)

links, 'hooks' picked up as mnemonics from one stanza to the next –
gheuanghen gheuen (1.3 and 2.1), *behaelde daer cleynen prijs* (4.4 and 5.7),
Blanck/blancker (3.7 and 4.2) – support the theory that the piece was
transmitted orally. The recurrence of rhyme sounds throughout the
song reinforces this interpretation.[19] The one surviving copy of the
song can, therefore, be seen as no more than an occasional
transcription of an oral text, continuously changing in time and place.
The language, too, is uncomplicated and would probably have been
more complex if the song were a product of art.

No other item in the *Antwerp songbook* includes such intense local
elements as this song. The most obvious are the deep sentiments of
urban pride, as well as the presence of 'Nieuwpoort' in almost every
stanza: 'For Nieuwpoort we want to fight' (1.5), 'Stand up ye burghers
of Nieuwpoort' (3.3), 'Nieuwpoort stand fast / Thou shalt not be
defeated' (4.6–7), 'That he had come without good counsel / Before
that city of Nieuwpoort' (5.5–6). At the end, the song unexpectedly
concludes with a wish for freedom in Flanders.[20] This, however, is
part of the 'poet stanza', which seems to have been added later on;
locals would have been more likely to sing about the protection of
Nieuwpoort. The stanza also asks the Virgin Mary for protection, who
held an important role as saviour in the culture of urban memory
concerning the siege. This might have been an intervention by a
commercially minded printer seeking to address a wider audience.

Crèvecoeur (stanzas 3 and 4) has a similar connection to local
memory. Of course, as leader of the French army he was part of the
story. However, in the memory of Nieuwpoort he seems to have
become the embodiment of the enemy. One tower of the city walls
was later named after Philippe de Crèvecoeur.[21] A final local part of
the song is in stanza 3, which is about Herman who rang the bells.
This Herman also seems to have given his name to a tower.[22] In the

---

[19] Paul Zumthor, *Introduction à la poésie orale* (Minneapolis: University of Minnesota
Press, 1990 1983]). I thank Dr David Murray for noticing some oral characteristics
such as the recurrence of rhyme sounds, especially *–oet* and *–ijs*.

[20] The earlier reference to Flanders is does not refer to the place but to the function
of the 'Sovereign-bailiff of Flanders', who joined the fight.

[21] The city accounts of 1527, 1536, and 1580 refer to 'the tower with the name
Crèvecoeur' (State Archive Bruges, Nieuwpoort City Archive, nos. 3616, 3626, 3667;
Vlietinck, *1489–1889: Eene bladzijde uit de geschiedenis der stad Nieupoort*, p. 68).

[22] In 1819, the local historian Rybens remarked that locally the city tower was called
'Hermanstorreken' (Herman's Tower) and was decorated with two statues, called
'Herman and his Son' (Rybens, *Beschryving der stad ende haven van Nieuport*, p. 369).
Antoon Viaene, 'Hermans Torreken te Nieuwpoort', *Biekorf*, 63 (1962), 217–18, linked
this detail to the song.

church archives of Nieuwpoort there are some registrations of a 'Herman Janssens' who was paid for restorations in 1488 and 1489.[23] Herman, therefore, might have been a sort of church contractor who saw the attackers and reacted by sounding the bells. These remarkable local elements indicate that the song originated in Nieuwpoort.

Other siege narratives

There is only the one song about the siege of Nieuwpoort, but other types of narratives about the siege survived. The source most cited is the chronicle of Jean Molinet, historiographer to the Burgundian court from 1475 until 1504.[24] His perspective is Burgundian, not local, and his loyalty is to the court. His chronicle was used as the main source of information about the siege, even shortly after he wrote it.[25] Another important source for the siege is one particular manuscript of the *Excellente Cronike* of Flanders, which probably originated in Nieuwpoort *c.*1494.[26] The 'Excellent Chronicle' is a tradition of manuscripts narrating a history of Flanders, most of them coloured by the wishes of the writer or commissioner of each manuscript. They are mostly brief when discussing the siege of Nieuwpoort, but this one manuscript has a very detailed account of the event.

The discourse in the song is extraordinarily similar to that of the *Excellente Cronike* manuscript, which takes a Nieuwpoort perspective and contains similar feelings of urban pride as well as numerous local details, some of which are also in the song, such as the ringing of the bells and a description of the drowned Swiss mercenaries. These are not found in Molinet's chronicle. The themes in the manuscript are likewise close to those of the song, such as treason and the possibility

---

[23] State Archive Bruges, Nieuwpoort City Archive, no. 3147, Church Accounts 1471–1490.

[24] For Molinet's account of the siege, see Georges Doutrepont and Omer Jodogne, *Chroniques de Jean Molinet*, 3 vols (Brussels: Palais des Académies, 1935–37), II, 138–41. On Molinet, see Jean Devaux, *Jean Molinet, indiciaire bourguignon* (Paris: Honoré Champion, 1996).

[25] Molinet was used as a main source for the siege in 1599 by Pontus Heuterus and in 1609 by Hareus, influencing further narratives. See Lori van Biervliet, 'Een oudt liedeken op het beleg van Nieuwpoort 1489', *Biekorf*, 76 (1975), 193–206.

[26] The Hague, Royal Library, MS 132A13, fols 520v–537v. See Lisa Demets, 'Onvoltooid verleden: Politiek, historiografie en de handschriftelijke variatie van de Excellente Cronike van Vlaenderen (1400–1550)' (unpublished doctoral thesis, Ghent University, 2019), pp. 265–78; Lisa Demets, 'The Late Medieval Manuscript Transmission of the Excellente Cronike van Vlaenderen in Urban Flanders', *The Medieval Low Countries*, 3 (2016), 123–73 (p. 172). Thanks to Lisa for sharing with me her knowledge and transcription of the manuscript.

of surrender. Molinet mentions these briefly, but stresses how the local women saved the city, which is not mentioned in the *Excellente Cronike* or in the song. Another significant difference is the person they hold responsible for the victory. The first four stanzas of the song are directed to the Sovereign-bailiff of Flanders, and the following two are probably his answer. The *Excellente Cronike* describes the Sovereign-bailiff as the hero of the siege. In addition, the city accounts show that the Sovereign-bailiff was thanked by the citizens several times.[27] In contrast, while the *Excellente Cronike* manuscript waxes lyrical on the subject of the Sovereign-bailiff, Molinet replaces him with the Mayor of Nieuwpoort, who has only a small role in the other sources.

The similarities between the song and the *Excellente Cronike* manuscript provide more evidence of local origin, they also confirm that the sense of victorious urban pride displayed in the song was current in Nieuwpoort shortly after the siege. And thanks to Molinet, we know that this was typical only of the local experience of the siege and not of writings about the siege in general.

Contrafacta: glimpses of reception

Contrafacta show glimpses of where and when a tune was known and of the social circles in which it circulated. Thus *contrafacta* add to the understanding of the overall reception of the Nieuwpoort song. They do not refer to the single surviving version, but rather to the tune as evidence of a dynamic, changing song. Textual parallels between *contrafacta* are also of importance as they emphasize the elements that stuck with the singers or the audience.[28]

Four *contrafacta* refer to the Nieuwpoort song in their tune directions. The oldest dates back to Nieuwpoort in 1511; the others are biblical, Reformation-inspired songs from quite a while after the siege and far away from Nieuwpoort. Finally, there is a political song that does not name the Nieuwpoort song as a tune direction but where there are good reasons to suspect a common melody.

---

[27] State Archive Bruges, Nieuwpoort City Archive, nos. 3586, 3599, City Accounts 1495, 1510.

[28] The mechanism of *contrafactum* has been studied for the Low Countries by Louis Peter Grijp, *Het nederlandse lied in de Gouden Eeuw* (Amsterdam: Meertens Instituut, 1991); Louis Peter Grijp and Dieuwke van der Poel, 'Introduction', in *Identity, Intertextuality, and Performance in Early Modern Song Culture*, ed. Dieuwke van der Poel, Louis Peter Grijp, and Wim van Anrooij (Leiden: Brill, 2016), pp. 1–38. Research on *contrafacta* is facilitated by the online database Nederlandse Liederenbank www.liederenbank.nl.

The earliest and most interesting *contrafactum* is a short song in a theatre play, *Maria ghecompareirt by de claerheyt* (*The Virgin Mary Compared to Clarity*), written by an early sixteenth-century rhetorician from Bruges, Cornelis Everaert, who, as well as being a prolific playwright, was a master fuller and dyer.[29] The play was staged in June 1511, as part of a competition held in Nieuwpoort between regional chambers of rhetoric, during the annual commemoration of the siege of Nieuwpoort.[30] It is therefore no coincidence that the short song in Everaert's play should have been set to the tune of the song about the siege.

In addition to the melody, the text of this short *contrafactum* refers to the siege and to our song. It praises the Virgin Mary, the guardian of the city, protecting 'us' from 'the enemy'. 'Clarity', to which the Virgin Mary is compared in the piece, refers to her purity as well as to the light of God. Throughout the whole year the citizens of Nieuwpoort kept burning a candle of the same length as the walls of the city, in fulfilment of a promise made when they were begging the Virgin Mary for assistance (to be the same length as the city walls, the candle was, of course, not a moulded candle but a wick rolled on a

'Al zynghende deze woorden up den voys van Nyeuport hout hu vaste ghy en sult niet ghevanghen zyn'	'Singing these words to the tune of Nyeuport stand fast thou shalt not be defeated'
Maria, edele vrauwe,	Mary, noble lady,
Ons alder toeverlaet,	Our refuge always,
Binnen sweerels landauwe	Within the world's fertile soils
Huwe oochskens up ons slaet.	Cast thine eyes upon us.
Ende als de doot ons leven hendt,	And when death ends our life,
In onser noot ons bystaet,	Help us in our agony,
Dat den vyant ons niet en scent.	So that the enemy does not ruin us.

(Hüsken, *De Spelen van Cornelis Everaert*, p. 748.)

---

[29] The text of the play iss preserved in an autograph of 1527, edited by Wim Hüsken, *De Spelen van Cornelis Everaert* (Hilversum: Verloren, 2005), pp. 747–84. For more about Everaert and his audience, see Wim Hüsken, 'Cornelis Everaert and the Community of Late Medieval Bruges', in *Drama and Community: People and Plays in Medieval Europe*, ed. Alan Hindley (Turnhour: Brepols, 1999), pp. 110–25.

[30] Vlietinck, *1489–1889: Eene bladzijde uit de geschiedenis der stad Nieupoort*, pp. 98–121. For more about these competitions, see Anne-Laure Van Bruaene, '"A Wonderfull Tryumfe, for the Wynnyng of a Pryse": Guilds, Ritual, Theater, and the Urban Network in the Southern Low Countries, ca. 1450–1650', *Renaissance Quarterly*, 59 (2006), 374–405.

spool).[31] At a certain moment in the play a nun appeared on stage explaining the meaning of 'clarity' in honour of Mary and carrying a candle.[32] In addition, the singer of the song in the play was blind, and the 'poet stanza' of our song describes the poet himself as a blind man.

While the actors were talking on the stage a blind man in the audience started singing this song to the tune of 'Nieuwpoort, hold steady'. While still singing, he climbed up on to the stage to join in the discussion. This man was, of course, an actor, but the audience was supposed to think he was one of them. The playwright used the melody of the Nieuwpoort song as a tool for including the urban audience in the action. The song must have been well known locally in 1511, and these links integrate the theatre play with the song in the culture of urban memory.

Besides the Everaert *contrafactum*, three different religious songs were written to the melody of 'Nieuwpoort hold steady': 'Paulus dat uutvercoren vat' (1552); 'O herders van syon coene' (1559); 'Christe bruydegom almachtich' (1582).[33] All three are biblical songs, a genre that flourished under the Reformation in the second half of the sixteenth century.[34] They were printed in places that were printing centres for Reformation ideas, as much as 200 kilometres from Nieuwpoort. These *contrafacta* were themselves well known for a long time; sometimes several copies survived, or a *contrafactum* itself had more *contrafacta*. Even though all these *contrafacta* come from similar social environments, the Nieuwpoort tune was more than a catchy melody that persisted in Reformation circles. Textual similarities between the Nieuwpoort song and the three biblical *contrafacta* show that not just the tune but the song itself was known to Reformers.

---

[31] See van Biervliet, 'Een oudt liedeken op het beleg van Nieuwpoort 1489', p. 198; Antoon Viaene, 'De lange kaars van Nieuwpoort en andere votiefkaarsen naar maat in de Middeleeuwen', *Biekorf*, 68 (1967), 257–69; Jan Dumolyn and Lisa Demets, 'La ville comme Sainte Vierge: Un aspect de l'idéologie urbaine en Flandre médiévale (fin du XIVe siècle-début du XVIe siècle)', *Cahiers électroniques d'histoire textuelle du LaMOP*, 9 (2016), 23–52.

[32] Hüsken, *De Spelen van Cornelis Everaert*, p. 757.

[33] See Nederlandse Liederenbank.

[34] Bert Hofman, *Liedekens vol gheestich confoort: Een bijdrage tot de kennis van de zestiende-eeuwse schriftuurlijke lyriek* (Hilversum : Verloren, 1993); Judith Pollmann, 'Singing for Reformation in the Sixteenth Century', in *Cultural Exchange in Early Modern Europe*, gen. ed. Robert Muchembled, 4 vols (Cambridge: Cambridge University Press, 2006–07), I, 294–316; L. P. Grijp, 'De honger naar Psalmen en schriftuurlijke liederen tijdens de Reformatie', in *Een muziekgeschiedenis der nederlanden*, ed. L. P. Grijp (Amsterdam: Amsterdam University Press, 2001), pp. 168–73.

The biblical *contrafacta* have a similar narrative structure to the Nieuwpoort song, starting with a dialogue between someone urging surrender and someone else encouraging resistance, and occasionally even the exact same words are used.

This suggests the song was used as a political signifier in Protestant circles. Which tune direction to use would have been a sensitive matter, and one would have expected that a biblical tune direction would have fitted a biblical song better than a secular one (in particular, Calvinists, among whom one of the *contrafacta* emerged, did not like to use secular melodies).[35] The singers retained the belligerent themes – the battle, the protection of the city, and the possibility of treason – from the Nieuwpoort song but replaced the substance with seemingly innocent biblical texts. In his study of *contrafactum* Grijp devotes a chapter to 'counterpart songs', songs that mockingly mirror other songs by keeping the form, melody, and content but establishing an essential contrast. This was not done just for fun, but for political reasons: for instance, songs could be composed to the melodies of an adversary's songs.[36] We can see these biblical *contrafacta* as political 'counterpart songs'. Religious dissidents took this opportunity subtly to play politics by means of melodic and textual references.

The last of these *contrafacta* is likewise a song with political connotations. It is part of a handwritten songbook compiled in 1517 by Antonius Ghyselers, who was probably a rhetorician from Mechelen, a city close to Antwerp.[37] This song was probably performed publicly and had a popular character similar to that of the Nieuwpoort song.[38] The songbook names a different tune direction, but the song shares the same unusual rhyme scheme and rhythm with

---

[35] Hofman, *Liedekens vol gheestich confoort*, pp. 162–247.

[36] See also Una McIlvenna, 'The Power of Music: The Significance of Contrafactum in Execution Ballads', *Past & Present*, 229 (2015), 47–89.

[37] The most recent transcription of this song can be found in Robert Michel, 'Het Handschrift-Ghyseleers' (unpublished master's thesis, Universiteit Antwerpen, 2000). A more accessible, though less correct, transcription is in Cornelia Catharina van de Graft, *Middelnederlandsche historieliederen* (Arnhem: Gysbers & Van Loon, 1904), pp. 121–23. Jan Frans Willems, *Oude vlaemsche liederen ten deele met de melodiën* (Ghent: F. en E. Gyselynck, 1848), p. 55, mentions two written chronicles of the city of Mechelen in the hand of Antonius Ghyselers. These manuscripts are now lost, but the poems that are thought to have been written by Ghyselers all have rhetorical characteristics.

[38] There are considerable differences between this song (and a few others) and other poems ascribed to Ghyselers that give a date of composition and are thus more likely to be from his own hand.

the Nieuwpoort song.[39] Additionally, some rhyme words and sounds prominent in the Nieuwpoort song recur here, such as *ghevanghen* and accented lines ending in *–oet*. The song comes from a time and place where the probability was high that the Nieuwpoort song was known.

The songs share other thematic and textual parallels. Both are pro-Habsburg. The Ghyselers song narrates the defence of a city, Hattem (300 kilometres from Nieuwpoort) in 1505. The opening lines are written from the standpoint of the anti-Habsburg forces, led by the Duke of Guelders, who (unlike in the Nieuwpoort song) were defending rather than attacking the city. The defenders are urged to surrender after a few nearby coastal cities have been taken, one of which is called the 'key of the coast', a phrase that had also been used of Nieuwpoort.[40] The line *hout u vaste* ('hold steady') is another element that appears in both songs.[41]

This same context of political revolt during the time of Emperor Maximilian points up a parallel between the two songs and strengthens the *contrafactum* hypothesis for the political significance of the Nieuwpoort tune. Was it a conscious choice to use the same melody?[42] Did the singers deliberately link the resistance of Nieuwpoort with the assault on Hattem? There is no place here to answer these questions. However, especially in combination with the evidence of the biblical songs, the melody seems to have gained a political significance on its way through the sixteenth-century Low Countries. The tune was never used as a *contrafactum* without textual parallels as well, which is unusual for *contrafacta* of the time.

* * *

The exceptional local elements in the Nieuwpoort song and its correspondence with the local narrative about the siege indicate that it did indeed originate in Nieuwpoort, as a victorious chant, probably sung by the burghers of the town. The song outlasted the first victorious decades and won a place in the urban memory, to be used

---

[39] The Nederlandse Liederenbank names this song as a possible *contrafactum* (also Martine de Bruin, email, 27 April 2018).

[40] Nieuwpoort is called 'key of the western quarter' in the city charter of 1494 (Vlietinck, *1489–1889: Eene bladzijde uit de geschiedenis der stad Nieupoort*, p. 30).

[41] The phrase is found again in an anti-Habsburg political song of the 1480s, but this song is lost, with only the two first stanzas preserved in references to it. See Herman Brinkman, *Dichten uit liefde: Literatuur in Leiden aan het einde van de Middeleeuwen* (Hilversum: Verloren, 1997), p. 56.

[42] The *contrafactum* could, of course, have been the other way round, or they could both be *contrafacta* of another, older song.

as a commemorative theatre piece. Further afield, the song played a role in the world of popular entertainments. That it was well known is evidenced both by its inclusion in the commercial *Antwerp Songbook* and by subsequent *contrafacta*. The song and its melody probably also acquired a political function. The *contrafacta*, which all refer textually to the original song, show how it became a musical symbol for the encouragement of a besieged city – on one the hand recycled for another pro-Habsburg song, and on the other parodied by anti-Habsburg Protestants. This case study demonstrates the evolution of a musical urban memory. The song's (mainly oral) path from siege to songbook, and the traces of public performance, reveal the popular experience of a political event in different stages and settings.

Cecil Sharp and the Rev. Charles Marson: The Early Years of Song Collecting in Somerset, August 1903–September 1905

DAVID SUTCLIFFE

The aim of this paper is twofold: to explore the connectivity between singers Cecil Sharp and Charles Marson visited in the course of their first seven Somerset field trips between August 1903 and September 1905, whether they met them through intermediaries, singer to singer referrals, or mere serendipity; and then to analyse how they recorded the singers, shedding light on their working relationship, primarily by scrutinizing the Field Notebooks Tunes (FNT) and Field Notebooks Words (FNW) held at the Vaughan Williams Memorial Library (VWML).[1] Sharp's fair copy books, Folk Tunes (FT) and Folk Words (FW), are held at Clare College, Cambridge. During the period in question Sharp and Marson met 111 singers and collected 588 song versions (*Figure 1*). They initially focused on two main locations in south Somerset.

1. Hambridge and the surrounding area, including Westport, Isle Brewers, Barrington, Shepton Beauchamp, and Ilminster – 34 singers, 230 songs

The story of Sharp's first encounter with folk song, the rendition of 'The Seeds of Love' by John England at Marson's vicarage in Hambridge on 22 August 1903, has been well reported.[2] The next few songs came rather randomly: the 'Wassail' song at Drayton,[3] 'Turnit-hoeing' at Long Sutton,[4] and 'Gossip Joan' sung by the ancient Job

---

[1] VWML, CJS1/9/1 (words), CJS1/9/2 (tunes). The field notebooks are cited by year and book number.

[2] Derek Schofield, 'Sowing the Seeds', *Folk Music Journal*, 8.4 (2004), 484–512.

[3] The 'visiting wassail' is a living tradition in Drayton village today and the song (FT 2) was probably sung by Miss Mary Quick (1885–1935), eldest daughter of the Rev. Henry Quick. Mary was working as a music teacher in Enfield in 1911.

[4] This drinking chorus song about the relentless task of hoeing turnip rows was hardly a major step forward for the would-be song collectors, but Sharp recorded it in full 'Zummerzet' dialect (FT 4). The singer, Charles Parsons (1869–1907), may have been recommended to Sharp by the Quick family, as he was raised by his uncle Charles Bishop in Drayton before moving to Long Sutton by 1901. Louie Hooper's version of the same song also includes Somerset dialect (FT 5).

Gillard.[5] In a lecture at the Hampstead Conservatoire, Sharp said that 'for the first week or so, our captures were few and of small account', but 'eventually we struck a rich vein of real Folk Song [. . .] and in the course of the next 10 days I took down over 40 songs'.[6] In a letter to Chloe Marson, Sharp said that he had already researched some of the new songs (probably at the British Museum) and was particularly pleased with his setting of 'The Sign of the Bonny Blue Bell' (FT 20), 'one of the Wednesday night captures'.[7] Allowing a week after he heard the 'Seeds of Love' on 22 August, and time for Sharp's researches in London, the date of 2 September 1903 seems most likely as the peak of this initial collecting bonanza.

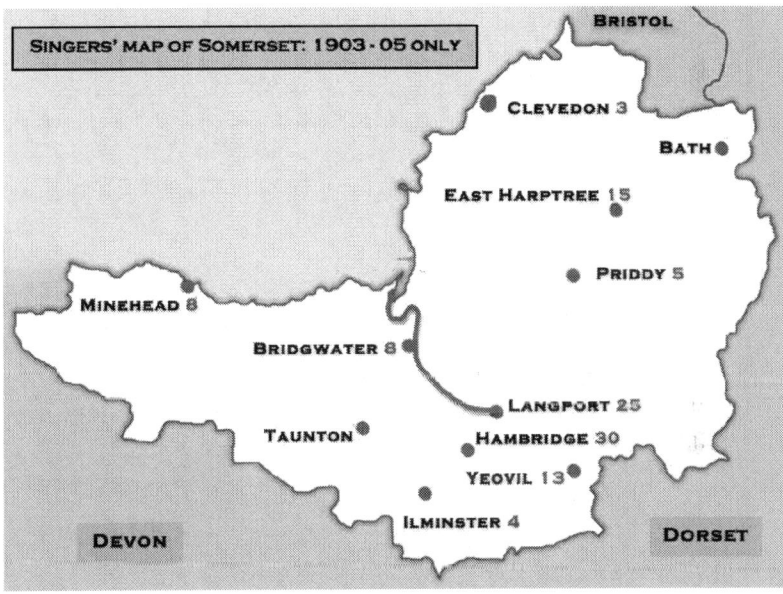

Figure 1
Distribution map of Somerset singers, 1903–05.

---

[5] Sharp recorded Job(y) Gillard's age as ninety-seven (FT 17). Sharp did not routinely write down singers' ages until the summer of 1905 but was evidently impressed with Gillard's longevity. Gillard was baptized at Drayton on Christmas Day 1810, but his exact date of birth is not known. He was recorded as a 'fisherman' in the censuses and may have known Marson through angling.
[6] VWML, CJS1/5/1, Lecture to Hampstead Conservatoire, November 1903, p. 17.
[7] VWML, CJS1/12/13/6/1, Sharp to Chloe Marson, 11 September 1903.

How did this come about? Marson wrote that the folk song adventure really began when 'one of the carters suggested that two or three women might help us' in the village.[8] The carter would probably have been William Ree, who worked with his younger brother Joseph at Hambridge Mill and Brewery.[9] William's wife Mary Jane (née Woodland, *b.*1862) was brought up in nearby Westport and knew both Lucy White and Louie Hooper well enough to recommend them as singers.[10] Much has, of course, been written about these two half-sisters (Lucy was fifty-four and Louie forty-three when they met Sharp), who contributed twenty-three of the forty or so songs that Sharp boasted about in his lecture.

Both Lucy and Louie had worked as glovers and shirt-makers, and were part of a wider network of home-workers. Gloving as a cottage industry seems to have been particularly conducive to the upkeep of folk songs. Women would often meet in small groups and sing to ease the relentless hours of hand-stitching in an intimate and supportive setting, with the opportunity to learn and repeat new songs. In an interview with the BBC in 1942, Louie Hooper said: 'I used to sit beside of the old women that used to glovey [*sic*] [. . .] and I used to do all I could to help them [. . .] I used to like to hear them sing and every word that they sing I tried to, you know, catch it from them. So that's where I learned all my songs, off of these old people.'[11]

The peak of the gloving industry was *c.*1870 and the centre of the trade was Yeovil with its tanning pits and nineteen glove factories.[12] Outworking in the surrounding villages was widespread, with glove agents distributing cut leather to be hand-stitched at home by an army of women workers.[13] Initially, the women were expected to walk to

---

[8] Cecil J. Sharp and Charles L. Marson (eds), *Folk Songs from Somerset* (London: Simpkin & Co.; Schott & Co. 1904), p. xiv.

[9] There were five other 'carters' recorded in the 1901 census. Two were newcomers to the village and three were young men without particular connections. William Ree (*b.*1859) had no songs himself, but his wife Mary Jane sang 'The Unquiet Grave', which was selected for the first series of *Folk Songs from Somerset*. Joseph Ree later sang two songs (FT 647, 648). Joseph's wife Sarah (FT 701) was John England's cousin.

[10] Mary Jane Ree's sister was Lizzie Welch (née Woodland, *b.*1868), who sang fifteen songs to Sharp and Marson in 1904.

[11] BBC, ref 6935, Lib no. 4039, 'Narration and Song False Love' transcript, 7 February 1942 (copy in VWML).

[12] *Kelly's Directory*, 1914.

[13] The American Singer sewing machine company did not set up its first small factory in Glasgow until 1867 but quickly expanded production in the 1870s and 1880s.

the distribution centres, often journeys of several miles.[14] One gloving agent, William Hawkins of Drayton, had two hundred women on his books in 1861.[15] The 'glove carrier' for Hambridge was John Brownsey, whose younger brother Charles opened the shirt factory in Westport when gloving dwindled in the 1880s. Many women easily transferred their skills to the new industry and learned to use sewing machines to assemble shirts, 'buttonhole' them, and produce detachable collars. A relative of Mrs Hooper reported that Sharp used to visit the factory to collect songs as the women worked.[16]

It is important to realize that to these singers folk song was a living thing, a part of their daily lives and a source of enjoyment and camaraderie. The average age of the Hambridge and Westport singers was just forty-four – the same age as both Sharp and Marson.[17]

2. Langport, Huish Episcopi and the surrounding area, including Drayton, Curry Rivel, and Muchelney – 25 singers, 172 songs

Family ties and occupational links may have assisted Sharp and Marson in and around Hambridge, but these factors did not apply when they ventured into the town of Langport in 1904. Geographical proximity to a 'singing pub' seems the likeliest link here: ten singers would be quickly found within 100 yards of the pub in question, the Railway Hotel.[18] This was in the busy west end of the town, near both the station and the riverside wharf.

Langport town was divided into All Saints' parish, bounded on the west by the River Parrett, and Huish Episcopi (St Mary's) up on the hill with its surrounding moors. The combined population in 1901 was 1,613.[19] The town was of a different order from the surrounding

---

[14] Report of Commission on the Employment of Women, Young Persons and Children in Agriculture (1867), HC4202-I (1868–9), XIII, 4/2.

[15] 1861 census, RG 9/1631, folio 67, p. 22.

[16] VWML, David Bland, Box 4, Folder 15, interview with Bill Adams (Louie Hooper's grandson), 16 September 1973: 'They used to have a shirt factory down the road. And he, Cecil Sharp, used to go in there and sit on the edge of the bench where my grandmother and they were working and as they sang, he'd take it down.'

[17] David Sutcliffe, Biographical Sketches, Part 1 (2019), a research project in draft form lodged at VWML, has identified all of the Hambridge singers, with their dates of birth, etc.

[18] The ten singers were: Emma Overd, Eliza Hutchings, Ellen Trott, Christopher Shire, Elizabeth Bray, Jane Perry, Alice Hull, Harriet Cattle (Kettle), John Hartland, and Maria Palmer. The last seven all lived along Bow Street (1901 census, RG13/2288, Langport District 1, pp. 3–9).

[19] In 1901, Langport had 813 people in its two census districts. Huish Episcopi had 706 people in its two districts. To these must be added the ninety-four people

villages with a bank, solicitor, physician, chemist, three bakers, three grocers, six dressmakers, five outfitters, two hairdressers, and a photographer. There were at least five beer-houses and five pubs.

Marson knew Langport well and Sharp used to arrive by train from London every holiday at Langport West station. Marson knew both vicars and it was probably through the Rev. Joseph Stubbs that Sharp and Marson met first Frederick Crossman of Huish Episcopi on 11 April 1904,[20] and Jane Wheller at the Langport Union Workhouse the following day.[21] Stubbs was the visiting chaplain at the workhouse, as it fell within his parish. The main breakthrough for songs, however, came later in the summer, on 30 July 1904, when Sharp met Mrs Emma Overd outside the Railway Hotel, originally called the New Inn (*Figure 2*).

The 'Lor, girls, here's my beau come at last' story has been told and retold,[22] but it might now be asked how Mrs Overd acquired her singing reputation and how Sharp first heard of it. In an interview with David Bland in 1974 Mrs Esther Overd (*b.*1906), daughter of Ellen Trott and wife of Herbert Overd, Emma's grandson, stated that Mrs Overd 'was known to go down every Friday to draw her OAP pension at the Post Office and then call in the Railway Hotel [. . .] if she had a half a pint or a pint [of beer], she'd sing'.[23] Evidently this was after Lloyd George's Pension Act of 1908, but Emma's singing reputation was long-lived. In the same interview Herbert Overd (*b.*1905) added that he could remember Emma 'dancing and singing, when she'd had a jar or two [. . .] She was a character, you know. Like many women she used to wear a man's flat cap.'

Emma Overd is supposed to have had an enormous repertoire of songs. She sang fifty for Sharp and Marson, and she could have sung more, but perhaps they were not what they were looking for. She may well have attracted the attention of George Adolphus Cox, who was

---

(including Mrs Overd) who lived in Langport Westover, technically part of Curry Rivel parish.

[20] Frederick Crossman (1845–1933) sang twelve songs over four visits. Marson was present on the first visit.

[21] Marson was present to notate all three of Jane's songs.

[22] A. H. Fox Strangways, in collaboration with Maud Karpeles, *Cecil Sharp* (London: Oxford University Press, 1933), p. 36. Fox Strangways and Karpeles were not, of course, present at the Overd encounter. The vicar's daughter who was present was probably Stubbs's daughter Ella (*b.*1876), as the Rev. David Ross, vicar of All Saints', Langport, had only two young boys at the time.

[23] VWML, David Bland, Box 6, Folder 3, interview with Mr and Mrs H. Overd, 6 March 1974.

the agent for the Somerset Trading Company and lived across the river from her. He was responsible for bringing in coal, timber, and other goods by both river and rail. The withy fields where Emma worked as a willow-peeler were within sight (and earshot) of Mr Cox's main depot at Bow Bridge.[24] Cox's help is acknowledged in the preface to the first series of *Folk Songs from Somerset* and he was clearly known to Marson. Cox and his two daughters took part in a concert organized by Marson at Hambridge in April 1904.[25]

Figure 2
The Railway Hotel, Langport (1940s).

Sharp's solo expeditions

Sharp set his own agenda separately from Marson from the very beginning. In April 1904, he found his own way to Muchelney village, four miles north-east of Hambridge, to discover Mrs Elizabeth Lock

---

[24] Mr Bob Clark, current owner of the property behind the Railway Hotel, personal communication. Remains were found of a withy shed that provided shelter for the twenty withy-strippers, who would boil the withy stems in the autumn months and then peel the bark off using a 'hand-brake' prior to their use in basket-making. The withy fields were still being cropped for hurdle-making until *c.*2010.
[25] George Adolphus Cox (*b.*1849) sang at Marson's concert (*Langport & Somerton Herald*, 30 April 1904). His daughter Ida Cox was listed as a music teacher in the 1911 census (RG14/14333, schedule 40).

(*b*.1839), who sang twenty-three songs for him over several visits. Sharp was introduced to her by another Muchelney resident, farmer's wife Mrs Amy Hunt (née Bryant). Amy's older brother, Dr John Bryant (*b*.1867), had become a prominent young physician at Guy's Hospital in London. He was Vice President of the Society of Somerset Men in London, which Sharp addressed in May 1904.[26] Dr Bryant sadly died in 1906,[27] but Sharp acknowledged the help of Mr and Mrs Hunt in the preface to the first series of *Folk Songs from Somerset*.

Sharp ventured upon several trips without Marson. One of the most significant of these solo trips was to the Mendip Hills for three days in April 1904 at the behest of William and Florence Kettlewell. They had heard through the local press of Sharp's appeal for folk songs,[28] and Sharp visited them at Harptree Court on eleven occasions over succeeding years. William Kettlewell had been in the army and had bought Harptree Court in 1875, the same year that he married Florence Olphert, who came from a wealthy Irish family. They were of liberal progressive views and took various initiatives in the village of East Harptree. Their eldest son, Henry (*b*.1876), later recalled in a letter to Sharp's biographer A. H. Fox Strangways that as a young man he had witnessed the speed with which Sharp worked:

> I can still clearly see in my mind's eye Cecil Sharp coming in after a long day's cycling over the Mendips with his notebook full of his curious musical short-hand notes and sitting down to the cottage Broadwood piano in the hall, piecing together and harmonising the airs he had collected.[29]

Sharp explored the Mendip Hills widely and met some inspirational singers. In an essay entitled 'The Mendip Singers' he singled out Farmer William King, Jim Bishop, John Vincent, Samuel Weeks, and Elizabeth Price for special praise.[30]

Sharp made important contacts with two clergymen during the 1904–05 period. One was the Rev. Frank Etherington, who hosted

---

[26] VWML, CJS1/5/2, Lecture to the Society of Somerset Men in London, May 1904.

[27] 'John Henry Bryant, M.D.Lond., F.R.C.P', *British Medical Journal*, 1 (1906), 1319–20.

[28] F. B. Kettlewell, *'Trinkum-Trinkums' of Fifty Years* (Taunton: Barnicott & Pearce, 1927), p. 61, refers to the *Bristol Times and Mirror* appeal for folk songs and her subsequent invitation to Sharp.

[29] VWML, CJS1/13/1/10/11, Henry Kettlewell to A. H. Fox Strangways, 11 October 1931. Henry Kettlewell's four children were all born in India between 1904 and 1908, so he probably witnessed Sharp at work in early 1904.

[30] VWML, CJS1/13/1/12/3, The Mendip Singers.

Sharp on frequent visits to west Somerset. Etherington was a Londoner who had known Charles and Chloe Marson in the late 1880s. He became vicar of Minehead in 1899, and introduced Sharp to Joanna Slade, a sailor's wife, who sang a full version of 'Claudy Banks', and then to Captain James Vickery and Captain Robert Lewis.[31] Vickery would eventually contribute nine songs and Lewis thirty-two.

A second and vital contact for Sharp was the Rev. William M. K. Warren, curate of Bridgwater. He had been in post since 1900 and was the visiting chaplain at the Union Workhouse, and introduced Sharp to two singers, Robert Dibble and George Radford. Bridgwater in 1901 was a busy town with a population of 15,168.[32] Access to the Bristol Channel brought in over three thousand ships in its peak year of 1885. New docks connected with both the Taunton & Bridgwater Canal and the Bristol to Exeter railway, opened in 1842. Hundreds of labourers worked on the docks and boatmen carried cargoes up the River Parrett to Langport. In addition, Bridgwater had a thriving brick and tile industry with over one thousand workers on sixteen sites, although conditions were harsh and there were several strikes in the 1880s. Bridgwater gave Sharp the opportunity to collect from male singers – thirty-two songs from seven singers.[33] From 1906 onwards he would greatly expand his work in Bridgwater, collecting a further 173 songs from thirty more singers. The final total for Bridgwater was 206 songs,[34] which represents 12 per cent of Sharp's total collecting in Somerset.

The field trips and recording practices

How were the songs 'recorded'?

First, some observations. It is invidious to compare one folk song collector with another in purely quantitative terms – numbers of songs

---

[31] FNW 1904/2.

[32] Philip J. Squibbs, *History of Bridgwater* (Chichester: Phillimore, 1982).

[33] The gender balance for the whole county for the first seven field trips (August 1903–September 1905) was 249 songs from sixty-three male singers (average 3.95 songs per singer), and 334 songs from forty-eight female singers (average 6.95 songs per singer). Five miscellaneous songs (supplied, for example, by correspondents) are excluded. The Bridgwater experience was the reverse. Admittedly over a longer time frame, the totals were 170 songs from twenty-five male singers (average 6.8 songs per singer), and thirty-six songs from thirteen female singers (average 2.8 songs per singer).

[34] Over many years, Sharp collected 227 tunes in Bridgwater, but fourteen of those were children's singing games and seven were checks on tunes previously collected.

and singers. Each collector tended to work a certain distinct territory; some worked steadily and thoughtfully over many years, while others worked in bursts of activity. Some had musical assistants; others happily accepted songs by correspondence. But nobody was quite like Sharp in terms of intensity and drive. With Marson's help, he attacked the enormous workload of the first two years with relish, but the overriding impression one gains from their field notebooks is that they were flying by the seat of their pants most of the time (*Table 1*).

Field Notebooks Words	Marson's handwriting	Sharp's handwriting	Marson's contribution
FNW 1904/1 April 1904	47 songs	26 songs	64%
FNW 1904/2 July–August 1904	39 songs	28 songs	58%
FNW 1904/3 August–September 1904	7 songs	55 songs	11%
FNW1904/4 December 1904–January 1905	–	24 songs	–
FNW 1905/1 August 1905	9 songs	39 songs	19%
FNW 1905/2 August–September 1905	15 songs	10 songs	60%
FNW 1905/3 April–August 1905	5 songs	63 songs	7%
Totals	122 songs	245 songs	33.2%

Table 1. Sharp and Marson's collaboration over the course of seven field trips.

For example, many songs were not initially recognized, so interim titles were entered, or no titles at all. Sharp took exclusive control of the field tunes notebooks, and in one of them, FNT 1904/9 (August 1904), there are forty-nine song entries of which twenty-two are untitled – a nightmare for the researcher. The situation is no better in the field words notebooks. In FNW 1905/1 (August 1905) seventeen out of twenty-seven song entries are untitled. Sharp was largely the culprit once more, but at least one can guess at a song from the words. Of course, it was difficult to catch a song 'from the lips of the singer', especially if the singer was nervous or suffered from a failing memory. One should not be too critical of human error, or of shortcuts when only certain stanzas or variations were recorded for songs that were already 'in the bag'.

In many instances, it took Sharp several attempts to pin down the musical structure of a song, with crossings-out, or variations in performance marked in particular bars. One has to remember that for both men this was their first experience of folk singing in the field and that they used the notebooks as a kind of *aide-mémoire* or shorthand to enable them to reproduce the songs in fair copy as soon as they feasibly could. They were learning on the job, and we should next examine how their work developed.

First field trip (August 1903)

We know about the forty-four songs collected during this short trip only from the fair copy books, because there are no field manuscripts extant. Sharp obviously took some working documents back to London and within a week he was working on arrangements for the sixteen songs that would be sung in his illustrated lecture at the Hampstead Conservatoire on 26 November 1903. Marson may have had his own copies of the songs (or else had outstanding recall), as he advised Sharp in a letter six weeks after the event that Louie Hooper certainly said 'He hath beguilèd me' in the first stanza of 'The Oak and the Ash' song.[35] It remains an open question as to how the words of all these early songs were safeguarded and entered with authority into Folk Words.

Second field trip (December 1903)

Perhaps in order to improve on their initial methods, Sharp began the second field trip in December 1903 with a brand new field notebook for tunes, which he alone would complete (FNT 1904/1). He and his wife Constance spent two weeks that Christmas at Hambridge vicarage. Their children aged nine, seven, five, and twenty-two months probably went with them, but Marson's wife and two children were away at the time. Marson was very busy with parish work over the Christmas period but he may have helped Sharp to record at least some of the forty-eight songs collected in Hambridge and nearby Isle Brewers village.[36]

---

[35] VWML, CJS1/12/13/7/3, Marson to Sharp, 13 October 1903. No song notes have survived among Marson's papers, archived at Taunton, Somerset Heritage Centre.

[36] For five years (1902–07) Marson covered Isle Brewers parish for its sick vicar, the Rev. John Cole. See David Sutcliffe, *The Keys of Heaven: The Life of Revd Charles Marson, Socialist Priest and Folk Song Collector* (Nottingham: Cockasnook Books, 2010), p. 269.

Sharp then left to visit the Rev. Alex de Gex at Meshaw Rectory in Devon, where forty more songs were collected in two more field notebooks.[37] It is unclear whether Constance went with him to Devon, but it was definitely she who transcribed fair copies from the field words notebooks, starting with Lucy White and Louie Hooper's 'Foggy Dew' from 23 December 1903 (FW 87), through the new Devon material, and right up to 'Limadee' (FW 307), a total of 168 entries. Perhaps Sharp had felt under pressure from all these songs stacking up in his notebooks. His handwriting can be seen (usually in red ink) on these pages, attributing singer's name and date, and cross-referencing songs to his Folk Tunes books, but the main texts are in Constance's handwriting – clearly a team effort at this early stage.

The recording system was quite imperfect, however. Eleven Somerset songs, from William Spearing, Lucy White, Louie Hooper, and others, appear in the fair copy Folk Tunes book but are not found in the field tunes notebook. Two of the eleven would later be published in the first series of *Folk Songs from Somerset*: 'The False Bride' and 'Poor Old Horse'.[38] The words of most of the eleven songs appear in full in Folk Words, so there must have been another source for them.

Third field trip (April 1904)

Sharp arrived at Hambridge on 4 April 1904 (Easter Monday) and had Marson's undivided attention for the next ten days, providing him with a new field words notebook in parallel with his own new tunes notebook. This may have been inspired by Sharp's sight of the Rev. Sabine Baring-Gould's three Personal Copy manuscripts, which had been kindly lent to him in January.[39] These were carefully laid out, with

---

Marson knew the villagers well and used to fish in the millpond of William Spearing, who contributed twenty songs.

[37] The Rev. Alex de Gex had contacted Sharp after attending the Hampstead lecture in London and invited him to visit him in Devon. Meshaw was close to the Taunton–Barnstaple railway line (now disused). FNT 1904/2 and 1904/3 are entirely devoted to Devon singers.

[38] FT 75, 77. The remaining songs not found in FNT 1904/1 are: FT 73, 74 'The Leaves' and 'Old Barn Door' (Spearman/Spearing); FT 76, 78, 79 'Chaps of Cocaigny', 'Joan's Ale', and 'Down by the Riverside' (Lucy White); FT 86 'Jolly Shilling' (Mr Mayle); FT 87 'Wassail Song' (Barrington Watzailers); FT 89 'Rosin the Beau' (Louie Hooper); FT 88 'Driving away with the Smoothing Iron' (Louie Hooper), which has just a chorus fragment in FNT.

[39] Martin Graebe, *As I Walked Out: Sabine Baring-Gould and the Search for the Folk Songs of Devon and Cornwall* (Oxford: Signal Books, 2017), p. 183, quotes Sharp's interview with

tunes usually on the left-hand page, words on the right. How would Sharp and Marson measure up to this new standard? In an intense period of activity over two weeks they collected seventy-three texts. Their entries in the field words notebook are readily distinguishable.[40] Marson generally used pencil and Sharp ink (*Figure 3*).

There was a man in Dover
He had a handsome wife
And she did love good company
So dear as she loved her life.
When this poor man came
home from work
'Twas late all in the night
Enquiring for his own dear wife
His joy & hearts delight.

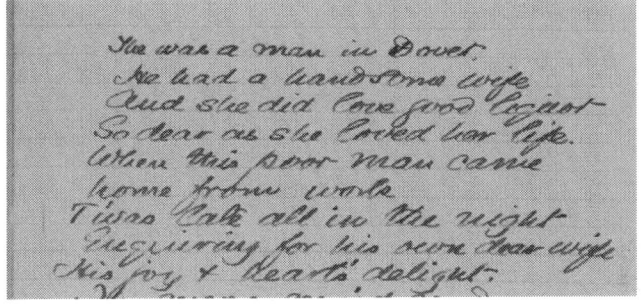

Figure 3a
'Man in Dover' taken down by Charles Marson (ink) (FNW 1904/1).

The Spotted Cow
Good morning fair maid where are you going
So early tell me now
She sighed & replied kind sir she said
I've lost my spotted cow
No longer weep no more complain
Your cow is not lost my dear
I saw it down in the yonder Grove
Come love and I'll show you where

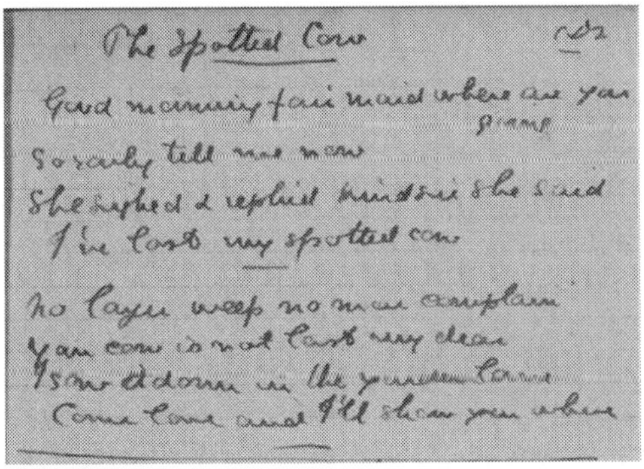

Figure 3b
'Spotted Cow' (taken down by Cecil Sharp (ink) (FNW 1904/1).

---

the *Morning Post*, 18 January 1904, in which he acknowledges the loan. Graebe believes the books were not returned to Baring-Gould until July 1904.

40 Four hundred of Marson's letters and papers are archived at Taunton, Somerset Heritage Centre, A\DFS M/3596, and the author is very familiar with Marson's handwriting.

Of the seventy-three texts collected that April, forty-seven were entered by Marson (64 per cent) and twenty-six by Sharp (36 per cent) (FNW 1904/1). It was Constance Sharp, however, who transcribed the field texts into the fair copy books. Four texts were deliberately dropped and not transcribed: 'Edwin in the Lowlands' (J. Ree), 'Soldier's Daughter' (Welch), 'Royal Albion' (Spearing), and 'Miller's Apprentice' (Welch).

In addition to these seventy-three texts, Sharp collected a further nineteen tunes on his own in Hambridge and in Harptree in the Mendips (FNT 1904/5), but failed to record the words in the field words notebook. The words for most of the songs are there in Folk Words, but once again the primary source is missing. Either a field notebook has gone astray or loose manuscripts have not survived.

Some of these nineteen tunes were picked up at the singing session held in the Castle of Comfort pub, near Priddy, on 15 April, as reported by Sharp five weeks later in his lecture to the Society of Somerset Men in London (CJS1/5/2):

> On Friday night [. . .] Mr K[ettlewell] drove me up to top of Mendip to 'Castle of Comfort' to which all the farmers and shepherds in the neighbourhood had been invited to sing [. . .] The majority of songs no use, but at last Farmer King [. . .] brought out this old Dorian melody ['Sheep Shearing' song].

It may have been difficult for Sharp to juggle two field notebooks in the close confines of the snug, but he did not record even rudimentary words for the 'Sheep Shearing' song in his field tunes notebook and one wonders how he reproduced it in time for it to be sung in London in May.

Two other important songs in this set of missing words were Louie Hooper's 'Broken Token' (FW 286) and William King's 'True Lover's Farewell' (FW 301), both of which would appear in the second series of *Folk Songs from Somerset* in December 1905.[41] Because

---

[41] The 'Broken Token' is a good example of how confusion can arise without clear provenance for a song. In FNT 1904/5, the tune 'I Have a Sweetheart of My Own' has no words attached to it and is attributed by Sharp to Lucy White, dated 13 April 1904. He transcribed this to FT 189 and re-titled it 'Broken Token'. Constance Sharp, working from a missing manuscript, transcribed three stanzas of words as FW 286, whereupon Sharp changed the title (again) and attributed the song to both Lucy White and Louie Hooper, with the same date of 13 April 1904. Unusually, Marson (in a footnote) then added an extra stanza from Louie Hooper and dated it 28 August 1905. There is, however, no corresponding entry in the field notebooks (words or tunes) for this extra stanza. When Sharp came to write notes for the song in Cecil J.

these two songs are transcribed in Constance's handwriting, and because she had (at least temporarily) given up transcribing by July 1904, one must assume that Sharp recovered the words from the singers very quickly, before new material could intervene.

Fourth field trip (summer 1904)

Sharp finished up one field tunes notebook (FNT 1904/5) with some good songs from a new singer, Harry Richards in Curry Rivel.[42] Marson collected the words for these in a new field words notebook (FNW 1904/2). Then Mrs Overd was contacted in Langport, with her many singing friends, and this was followed by the trip to Minehead, which is when a few glitches begin.

There is no record in the field words notebook of the distinctive 'Two Magicians' song by Minehead blacksmith William Sparks. It is there in the field tunes notebook, entitled 'The Coal Black Smith', but the song must have been reconstructed from other sources for publication.[43] More missing words occur with 'Tarry Trousers' (Anna Pond, Shepton Beauchamp, 16 August 1904) (FW 406) and 'Lord Rendal' (Louie Hooper, Hambridge, 18 August 1904) (FW 445–446). Both are found in Folk Words but are not present in the field words notebooks.

In the final week of August, Constance Sharp helped out by transcribing the words to twelve more songs (FW 467–479). *Figure 4* overleaf shows the differences in their handwriting: several letters are differently formed, in particular capital 'F' and 'I', and Cecil's rigid 'y'.[44]

Sharp and Charles L. Marson (eds), *Folk Songs from Somerset*, 2nd series (London: Simpkin & Co.; Schott & Co. 1905), p. 71, he attributed the six-stanza song to Louie Hooper, writing that 'Hooper's version was very incomplete, so Mr Marson has made free use of the broadside verses'. But the tune Sharp used was actually the original tune Lucy White sang in 1904, albeit with the key transposed from D to A and with adjusted metre.

[42] 'Erin's Lovely Home', 'Just as the Tide was Flowing', and 'Trees They Do Grow High' would all be selected for *Folk Songs from Somerset*.

[43] 'Two Magicians', William Sparks's only song, appeared in *Folk Songs from Somerset* (1st series, no. 19). The melody only is in FNT 1904/5. It was not collected anywhere else in the county.

[44] Constance Sharp's handwriting is consistently smaller than Cecil's. Two further samples of her writing are in Taunton, Somerset Heritage Centre, A\DFS M/3596, letters 349 and 356. (*Note*: VWML, CJS1/12/13/6/4, is an extract in a third-party hand of a letter from Constance Sharp to Chloe Marson dated 26 January 1909.)

Fifth field trip (December 1904)

This was a less prolific holiday for Sharp. He spent a week in Hambridge, a week in Devon, and a week in Harptree. He collected just twenty-nine songs in Somerset, but they included two good songs, 'Dabbling in the Dew' and 'Earl Richard', from Jack Swain, a shepherd at Donyatt, near Ilminster, who was understandably upset by Sharp's unannounced visit on Christmas Day.[45]

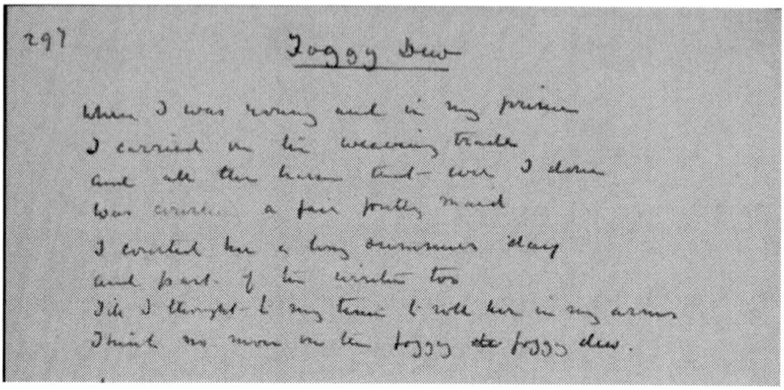

297 Foggy Dew

When I was young and in my prime
I carried on the weaving trade
And all the harm that ever I done
Was courting a fair pretty maid
I courted her a long summer's day
And part of the winter too
Till I thought to my time to roll her in my arms
Think no more on the foggy dew the foggy dew.

Figure 4a
FW 297: 'Foggy Dew', Constance Sharp's handwriting.

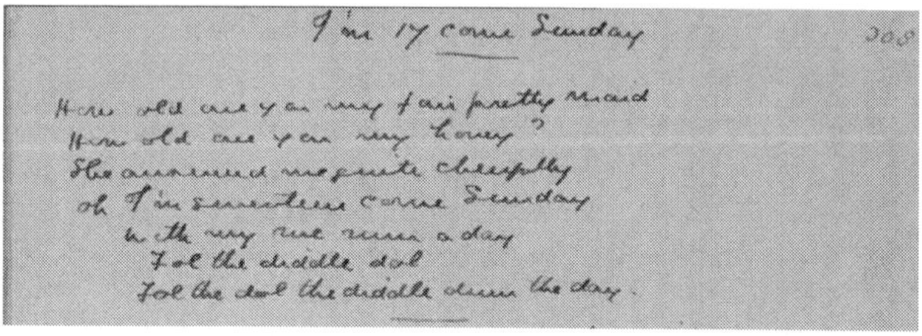

I'm 17 come Sunday 308

How old are you my fair pretty maid
How old are you my honey?
She answered me quite cheerfully
Oh I'm seventeen come Sunday
With my rue rum a day
Fol the diddle dol
Fol the dol the diddle dum the day.

Figure 4b
FW 308: 'Seventeen Come Sunday', Cecil Sharp's handwriting.

Sixth field trip (Easter 1905)

This was another quiet episode, with only eighteen songs collected in April 1905.

[45] Both were properly recorded in both field notebooks, and both appeared in *Folk Songs from Somerset* (2nd series).

Seventh field trip (summer 1905)

In the summer of 1905, Sharp explored the Yeovil area, including Haselbury Plucknett and Merriott, and collected thirty-three songs. Then he collected thirty-one songs in Bridgwater town. Finally he met Samuel Weeks and Jim Bishop at Priddy. Marson helped when he could.

Transcription from field notebooks to fair copies

Although there are gaps in the overall record of data collection, it is important to comment positively on the very close affinity between the records in the field words notebooks and in Folk Words. The words were transcribed into fair copy with absolute fidelity, with no attempt to eliminate dialect words or to tidy up grammar. A few examples will suffice. Jack Swain in 'Dabbling in the Dew' sang, 'Oh the divil would fitch me back again', a dialect phrase that is perfectly replicated in Folk Words (FNW 1904/4, FW 569–570). In 'Brimbledown Fair', Jim Woodland sang of pretty Nancy 'a curdling her hair', again reproduced exactly (FNW 1904/1, FW 241). Marson's record of the 'naughty' verses of Harry Richards's 'Just as the Tide Was a Flowing' is there in its entirety (FNW 1904/2; FW 318–320), although a whole stanza would be omitted when published in *Folk Songs from Somerset*. [46]

The transfer of songs from field notebooks to fair copies could have been random and haphazard, but it was not. There are certainly occasional examples of songs out of sequence, but the general pattern is that the tunes took precedence as the leading indicator and the words followed in sequence. Sharp took absolute control of the fair copy work, cross-referencing painstakingly from tune to words. Even with a computer database, it is very difficult to keep on top of the data. The speed with which Sharp proceeded is confirmed by a letter to Marson dated 18 February 1906 in which he wrote that (despite a bout of influenza) he had 'used my spare time in working away at indexing songs [. . .] and harmonising for 3rd series'.[47]

* * *

The field notebooks are an insufficient source for all the early Somerset songs. The words to at least thirty songs are not found in

---

[46] *Folk Songs from Somerset* (2nd series, no. 37).

[47] Sharp's letter of 18 February 1906 is among Marson's papers in Taunton, Somerset Heritage Centre, A\DFS M/3596, letter 303. Sharp had only finished song collecting on 23 January 1906.

the field notebooks, so some manuscripts must be missing. There is no reason, however, to doubt the integrity of Sharp and Marson's compilation. They both honestly admitted when they borrowed words from broadsides or from other singers in order to make a song work. Their treatment of certain words for publication, however, is another matter.

Marson's role in taking down one third of the song words over this first period of collaboration is significant. Sharp highly valued the sharing with Marson of both the workload and the enjoyment of the project. Constance Sharp's role in transcribing 180 of the early song entries (139 from Somerset and forty-one from Devon) is also significant. The fidelity of transcription from field notebooks to fair copies was very high. When Sharp left Hambridge to explore Bridgwater, Sedgemoor, and Exmoor in 1906, Marson hardly contributed at all. It is not surprising that the two men fell out in November of that year after a personal spat.